EVOLUTION AND
CHRISTIAN FAITH

EVOLUTION AND CHRISTIAN FAITH

BY H. H. LANE
PROFESSOR OF ZOOLOGY
UNIVERSITY OF KANSAS

WIPF & STOCK · Eugene, Oregon

Wipf and Stock Publishers
199 W 8th Ave, Suite 3
Eugene, OR 97401

Evolution and Christian Faith
By Lane, H. H.
ISBN 13: 978-1-61097-444-8
Publication date 4/20/2011
Previously published by Princeton University Press, 1923

TO MY WIFE

*Whose Interest and Understanding
Have been an Unfailing Stimulus
in the Writing of this Book*

PREFACE

THIS book has grown out of a course of lectures prepared and delivered in response to the following petition:

We, the undersigned students of this University,* respectfully request that you give us a course of lectures setting forth

I.
What is the theory of evolution and what are the important facts on which it is based; and

II.
What effect the acceptance of that theory has upon one's views of the Biblical account of creation and of the Christian Religion.

The events of the past year or two show clearly that not only the students in our colleges and universities, but many people outside of those institutions as well, are seeking the answer to these questions. For the most part, those who have attempted to throw light on the problem have been those who are either too ignorant scientifically to speak with authority, in which case the most absurd and sensational fulminations have been pub-

* Phillips University.

Preface

lished, which only befuddle or disgust the mind of the serious, thoughtful seeker for the truth, or else, the authors, while scientifically competent, have not been, as a rule, exactly aware of the difficulties confronting the student mind.

Owing to more than forty years' familiarity with the thought and belief of Christians in general, partly due to his boyhood and youth spent as the son of a devout minister of the Gospel, partly because of over thirty years' membership in an evangelical body of Protestantism, during which time he has served in practically every church office open to a layman, partly on account of his experience as a student in five universities (DePauw, Indiana, Cornell, Chicago, and Princeton), and partly through a teaching experience as professor of zoology in four colleges and universities, two of them under church control and two important state universities, the author feels that he has had peculiar opportunities to approach the questions with a clear understanding of both sides of the controversy.

No effort has been made to write anything strictly new or distinctly original; the problem in hand is so definite and presses so hard for solution that the author has drawn freely upon all available sources. He therefore acknowledges his great indebtedness to the work of many writers, not all of whom can be listed here. But especial acknowledgments are due to Professor E. G. Conklin, of Princeton University, for the general plan and many of the facts given in the chapter on the

PREFACE

Embryology of the Mind; to Professor H. V. Neal, of Tufts College, for the same in regard to the chapter on the Problem of Ultimate Causation; while to the works of the late Professor Joseph LeConte, the author is under obligations for numerous ideas embodied here and there throughout the whole book. A number of lesser debts are acknowledged by quotation marks and references throughout the text.

This book has been written to meet the need of the man or woman who is troubled by the idea, unfortunately so prevalent, that acceptance of the results of modern science involves the repudiation of long-cherished religious beliefs. It is intended to show more especially that the biological doctrine of evolution does not preclude faith in the Divine Power that operates in and through the universe, but rather inforces such a faith. It is an attempt at an interpretation of reality compatible with idealistic realism and in opposition to the philosophic materialism so frequently adopted by those who wish to be "abreast of the times." The author sincerely hopes that it may remove some of the obstacles which have kept many minds from a belief in the possibility of that deepest need of the human soul—a religious faith.

H. H. LANE

July 22 1922

CONTENTS

PREFACE		*Page* vii
I.	INTRODUCTION	1
II.	THE SO-CALLED WARFARE OF SCIENCE AND THEOLOGY	9

PART I: SCIENCE

III.	THE FACT OF EVOLUTION	23
IV.	HAS MAN EVOLVED?	53
V.	THE GEOLOGICAL HISTORY OF MAN	67
VI.	THE ROLE OF THE HAND IN THE EVOLUTION OF MAN	81
VII.	SOME DISADVANTAGES OF THE UPRIGHT POSITION	91
VIII.	THE EMBRYOLOGY OF THE MIND	99

PART II: PHILOSOPHY

IX.	THE PROBLEM OF ULTIMATE CAUSATION	125
X.	THE ORIGIN OF THE INDIVIDUAL *VERSUS* THE ORIGIN OF THE SPECIES	145
XI.	WHAT AND WHERE IS GOD?	155
XII.	EVOLUTION AND GENESIS	173
XIII.	EVOLUTION AND CHRISTIANITY	187
XIV.	THE SWING OF THE PENDULUM	201
SUGGESTED READINGS		213

CHAPTER I

INTRODUCTION

UPON the publication of Darwin's "Origin of Species," and more particularly of his later work on "The Descent of Man," there arose a fierce controversy between the more militant scientists and the theologians, which lasted for many years. By the beginning of the twentieth century this controversy had subsided to such an extent that it no longer attracted general interest or attention. The result was construed by scientists generally as favorable to their point of view since many theologians had either openly accepted the scientific position or else made little noise with their opposition. Of recent years it has been frequently asserted in scientific circles that the battle was ended and that probably never again would it be revived. In the majority of the more important institutions of learning the doctrine of evolution is tacitly assumed in nearly all departments and frequently little or no attempt is made to evaluate the evidence on which the doctrine rests nor to examine its philosophical implications.

More recently, however, the fire of opposition to the doctrine of evolution, or, more particularly, to certain theories advanced in connection with it, has flamed up anew. Especially is this true in certain colleges conducted under the auspices of various religious denominations, and likewise on the part of several well-known public speakers, ministerial and otherwise.

This recrudescence of the old conflict is due to several causes, the first of which is perhaps a general misunderstanding of the aim and scope of science. Too frequently theories and conclusions which belong rather in the field of speculative philosophy have been mistaken by the unthinking or uninformed for theories or conclusions of science. It cannot be denied that in some cases the scientists themselves are largely to blame for this situation since they have not always been careful to make clear distinctions between their scientific facts and their philosophical deductions. It cannot be too emphatically stated that science is merely the orderly arrangement of facts or phenomena arrived at by observation or experiment in the realms of matter and energy. The scientist, as such, is limited to the consideration of those phenomena of the universe which are measurable or ponderable, and to the sequential relations discovered to exist among them. He is, therefore, limited in his scope to the discovery of *proximate* causes. He can never, as a scientist, deal with *ultimate causation;* that subject belongs to philosophy and not to science. Yet, because some eminent scientists have turned philosophers and, more especially, because they have then sometimes advocated a materialistic philosophy, the non-

INTRODUCTION

scientific public has generally concluded that all science is materialistic in tendency. The real truth is far from this common belief, but because there is more sensation in a heterodox doctrine, the public has become duly acquainted with the works of such men as Haeckel, while the more numerous but less sensational, because more orthodox, authors have been largely passed by with little notice or acclaim.

Another reason for the present situation is to be found in the fact that the philosophizing scientist with materialistic tendencies has been more prone to publish his views than have been those opposed in position. Especially has it been true that in the fields of psychology, sociology, and pedagogy, many brilliant, but philosophically immature authors have gone to wholly unwarranted extremes in their advocacy of the materialistic position in philosophy; have apparently taken delight in deriding the doctrines of the Christian religion; and have striven to impress the idea that all science supports their doctrines or theories, no matter how extreme they may be. The effects of such teaching upon the impressionable minds of high school or immature college students could not but have most unfortunate results. It is not surprising therefore that a respectable proportion of the general public, especially of those who are alert to the maladies and dangers now threatening the body politic, should have become alarmed at the prospect; that in their ignorance of the true situation they should have so frequently mistaken the real source of the danger, is not to be wondered at. With the end which the sincere opponents of these doctrines are striving to attain, most thoughtful scientists are in complete sympathy. They differ only in their views as to the correct means to be used in combating the unwarranted doctrines of the extremists on the other side.

Directly or indirectly, the extreme views of the materialistic philosophers have a most deleterious effect, first upon the attitude of mind of the young or thoughtless student toward law, morality and religion, and in the second place, when widely held, they may even bring about international discord, and national immorality as was recently clearly indicated by the behavior of a great but materially minded country of Europe. Scientists themselves, it may be stated without the possibility of successful contradiction, have been among the first and foremost to issue warnings against the unwarranted conclusions of those who attempt to base a philosophy of life, both national and individual, upon a partial or improper view of scientific facts and doctrines. Perhaps because of the scientist's usual propensity to consider things quietly and judiciously, without a violent display of emotion, the warnings have fallen on unheeding ears. Few scientists have the temperament that seems to characterize a public reformer; but there is the possibility that on this very account the doctrines which they advocate, in the long run shall prevail.

INTRODUCTION

That the majority of mature scientists are materialists is a wide-spread belief which is not substantiated upon proper examination of the facts. Statements based upon the results of questionnaires or other means of determining the philosophical or religious beliefs of scientists are usually misleading, partly because of their incompleteness and partly because of bias in the interpretations. A far better idea of the scientific attitude may be obtained from the published works of recognized leaders in science. Space forbids more than one illustrative quotation, taken from J. Arthur Thomson's "Introduction to Science":

"Nor can it be said that Science engenders an irreverent spirit; the biographies of all the greatest scientific investigators show the reverse. The irreverent and the unwondering are to be found among those who know least, not among those who know most. It is true that minor mysteries disappear, or, at least, that they cease to be mysterious in a superficial way, but it has been the experience of many a student of Science that when the half-gods go the gods arrive" (p. 213).

Again the same author says:

"In face of the often terrible failure of human endeavor, the element of tragedy in things as they are, and the chill that follows the vision of our fair earth and all that it contains becoming cold and cindery as the moon, many a one of great repute in the world of Science—we think of men like Clerk Maxwell or Kelvin—seeks to steady himself in the thought of some Abiding Reality, saying as of yore, 'I will lift up mine eyes unto the hills' " (p. 200).

In the discussion that occupies the succeeding pages the author has attempted to maintain the scientific attitude of mind, which consists in an honest endeavor to receive the truth whatever its nature and source, in a determination to secure all facts essential to the question at issue, with the intention of testing every hypothesis by application to further facts and relations, discarding each hypothesis whenever it becomes untenable by reason of contradictory phenomena, and of arriving at final judgments only when there seems no escape from them; in a spirit of tolerance for the opinions of others whether in accord or in disagreement with his own, a spirit which seeks to account for them rather than to ridicule or denounce them; in short, with a freedom from acrimony, blind partisanship and prejudice to seek the truth that makes men free.

This scientific attitude of mind will be enforced by the scientific method, the method which proceeds first to the collection of relevant data and the evaluation of the same, and then to the orderly arrangement and classification of the facts secured, analyzing them and reducing them to their simplest terms, in order to deduce from them their proper sequences. Such a discovered relationship constitutes a "natural law," the statement of which is one of the ends and aims of science.

One of the most important results of scientific procedure in the past has been the discovery of that fundamental law of nature, namely, its uniformity. This postulate has been subjected to innumerable tests of observation and experiment, of every conceivable kind, in nature and in the laboratory, until it has come to stand upon an apparently impregnable foundation. This means that so far as scientific experience has gone every event in nature stands as the end of a series of antecedent events which constitute its proximate causes. The universality of the law of cause and effect is so generally recognized that it is not necessary to dwell on it further here.

CHAPTER II

THE SO-CALLED WARFARE OF SCIENCE AND THEOLOGY

IT has been the fashion in some quarters to speak of a conflict between science and religion. It is commonly believed and sometimes taught that in this conflict religion has been uniformly defeated and discredited. This is far from being the case. The fact is that with a proper understanding of the terms, science and religion, there not only has never been but there cannot be a conflict between the two. Each term stands for a system of knowledge differing from the other, but both equally true and neither contradictory. Recognizing these facts, some have amended the statement to read, "The Conflict Between Science and Theology," seeking to distinguish between the essential elements of true religion and any dogmatic theories or beliefs regarding it. The blame is shifted to the shoulders of professional churchmen, sometimes Roman Catholic, sometimes Protestant as the case may be. But a candid examination of the facts may put the matter in a somewhat different light still.

Six great conflicts have occurred in this so-called "war between science and theology." The first of these was upon the question of the shape of the earth and its relation to the heavenly bodies. Primitive man, limited in knowledge and experience, looked about him and proclaimed the earth to be flat. He turned his eyes upward to the sky and circled the horizon with his vision, and declared that the earth is covered with a canopy or tent. Noting the sun, moon and stars apparently hanging from this canopy like so many lamps, and noting their apparent diurnal movements, he concluded that the canopy of the sky moves from east to west overhead. Considering the means which primitive man possessed for testing his hypothesis, this was really a *scientific* theory. It gave a satisfactory explanation for all the astronomical phenemena which he could observe. For many centuries no better theory was advanced and no knowledge accumulated to contradict it. The Greeks later perceived that the contrary theory of the sphericity of the earth and its daily revolution on its axis would equally well account for the facts, but they were in no position to prove it.

The early church fathers apparently were unconcerned as regards these two rival theories, some held to the one, some to the other, with no apparent difference in respect to their reputations for orthodoxy. This indifference was due to the fact that the church had weightier matters in hand than to decide a purely scientific question. In the sixth century an Egyptian monk, Cosmas Indicopleustes, is said to have supported the theory of a flat earth by an appeal to Scripture, but in the

SCIENCE AND THEOLOGY

seventh century we find Isidore of Seville, and in the eighth, the Venerable Bede, both declaring their belief in the earth's sphericity. Not until Magellan's circumnavigation of the globe in the sixteenth century was the matter put to the test of scientific demonstration. It is hard to see how this "conflict" can be truly ascribed to a warfare between science and theology. It was, as always, a conflict between knowledge and ignorance, and it was settled only when knowledge, *i.e., science,* became sufficiently complete as to be definite and irrefutable.

However, the observations of the Saracen astronomers; the experience of sailors regarding the appearance and disappearance of ships at the horizon; the shadow of the earth on the moon at its eclipse; these, and other things, made such an impression upon the mind of Columbus that he concluded he could reach India by sailing westward over the Atlantic Ocean. But when he undertook to interest men of vision and of wealth in his project, he was long baffled and rebuffed. The whole scientific authority of his day was against him; practical men of affairs decided, rightly enough in the light that they possessed, that his proposition was chimerical and promised no return for the investment of hard-earned wealth. In the meantime the Church had accepted the current scientific theory of the astronomers, and had found Scriptural grounds for its support. So long and so generally accepted had the theory of a *flat earth* become, that the theology of the day had adjusted itself to it. Hence it is not surprising to find that there were those ready to point out the "irreligious" tendency of the Columbian proposition, nor that it was even formally condemned by the Council of Salamanca on the ground that it was contrary to the Pentateuch, the Psalms, the Prophecies, the Gospels, the Epistles, as well as the writings of such early fathers as St. Chrysostom, St. Augustine, St. Jerome, St. Gregory, St. Basil and St. Ambrose. Was this really a conflict between science and theology? Was not the "science" of the day wholly in accord with the Church? Or rather, was not the theological dogma based upon the current scientific hypothesis? A candid historian must conclude that here was but one of the many conflicts between *rival scientific theories,* neither of which had yet been definitely proven.

The second "conflict" arose over the question of the *geocentric* versus the *heliocentric* theory of the solar system. According to the former, the earth occupies the center of the universe and in succession there revolve around her the moon, Mercury, Venus, the Sun, Mars, Jupiter, and Saturn; beyond the orbit of Saturn was thought to be the "firmament" of fixed stars. This was the generally accepted *scientific* theory of European astronomers until the discoveries of Galileo in 1610. According to the *heliocentric* theory, the sun is the center of the solar system and the earth is but one of the several planets which revolve around it.

In 1543 Copernicus published his great work

SCIENCE AND THEOLOGY

"On the Revolutions of the Heavenly Bodies," in which he developed the heliocentric theory into a scientific hypothesis, strictly true as regards its general outlines, but now demonstrably in error as regards many details. It was merely a hypothesis, however brilliant, and was not proven until the discoveries of Galileo in 1610 put it upon a firm foundation. It is true that Copernicus had delayed the publication of his hypothesis for thirty-six years out of fear for his own personal safety, and it was perhaps well for him that the first printed copy was placed in his hands while he lay upon his death-bed, for the Inquisition condemned it as heretical and utterly contrary to the Scriptures. This was not done, however, until after consultation had been held with the supposedly best astronomers of the day, who had pronounced the heliocentric theory as wholly without scientific foundation. Again it is clear that the conflict was not between the astronomical science of that day and the Church, so much as between rival scientific hypotheses.

During the second and third decades of the seventeenth century, *i.e.*, from about 1609 to 1632, Galileo was studying the heavens with his newly invented telescope, made with his own hands. With this crude instrument he discovered that the face of the moon, just like the earth, is dotted with mountain peaks and valleys; that the sun revolves on its own axis and has its lustre dimmed by spots; that the planets, including the earth, likewise revolve on their own axes and circle around the sun in definite orbits; these and many other discoveries attesting the truth of the Copernican hypothesis were revealed by that crude set of lenses in Galileo's hands and caused profound alarm in the ranks of astronomers and churchmen alike. The low and ignorant denounced these discoveries as frauds and deliberate deceptions. Some, apparently seeking to be more fair-minded, affirmed that, while the telescope might be all right when used as a spy-glass to view distant objects here on earth, with the heavenly bodies it was altogether a different matter and not to be relied upon. Note that these were the opinions of the leading astronomers as well as the theologians of the time. Considering this fact as well as the stage of civilization then attained, and the prominent place occupied by theological dogma in the affairs of both church and state, is it a matter for surprise that charges of "imposture, heresy, blasphemy, and atheism" were brought against Galileo? It was clearly a conflict between newly established knowledge and long and generally accepted ignorance. Galileo was a leader in thought far in advance of his time and suffered the fate which has almost uniformly been meted out to those who have the temerity to go counter to the beliefs of the ignorant and uninformed in positions of power and authority, whether the matters involved be questions political, moral, or religious in nature.

Simple minded scientist that he was, conscious of the absolute correctness of his views, Galileo thought to vindicate himself against such charges in a letter to the Abbé Costelli, in which he suggested "that the Scriptures were never intended to be a scientific authority, but only a moral guide." Far from pouring oil on the troubled waters, this letter succeeded only in setting fire to the oil, and he was summoned before the Holy Inquisition under the indictment that he taught the movement of the earth around the sun, a doctrine affirmed by his persecutors to be "utterly contrary to the Scriptures." He was compelled to renounce his heresy on pain of imprisonment. This was in 1616, and as he was then more interested in a further study of the heavens through his telescope than he was in the delights of life in a Roman prison cell, he complied with the decree, denounced his teaching, but is said to have muttered to himself as he left the presence of the judges, "But the earth does move just the same!"

Sixteen years later, in 1632, he published his noted work, "The System of the World," in which he set forth his evidence in support of the Copernican hypothesis. Once again he was brought before the Inquisition at Rome, accused of heresy in that he had asserted the revolution of the earth around the sun, and was convicted. He was first compelled, on his knees and with his hand upon the Bible, to abjure and curse his doctrine of the movement of the earth around the sun, and then, because of its being a second offense, he was thrown into prison, treated with all the severity which his remorseless persecutors could devise, for the remaining ten years of his life, and after his death the punishment was prolonged forever by denying him burial in consecrated ground.

Painful as the contemplation of these details may be, still it is clear that the persecution of Galileo is to be credited not so much to theology as to the state of civilization in which he chanced to live. It was an age in which ignorance and superstition were rampant; an age in which kings and popes could boast less real knowledge in most lines than that possessed by the average ten year old child of today. It was an age in which the doctrine of love and charity had had but little development. While in one sense the Church was responsible, in another and truer sense, the churchmen did but reflect the character of the times. No stream rises higher than its source, and so long as ignorance was the lot of even the leaders of the day, so long as the knowledge that comes from accurate, painstaking investigation of nature had not been acquired save by the exceptional man like Galileo, so long might such scenes as that just described, be expected. The conflict, be it emphasized, was not so much between science and theology, as between science and ignorance. Looking back through the light of the present day knowledge one may be inclined at first to charge the Church with inexcusable slowness in seeing the truth and accepting it. In reality the churchmen were more interested in speculative theology than in a knowledge of natural phenomena. They simply accepted the pseudo-science of their day in so far as it seemed to harmonize with their dogmas.

SCIENCE AND THEOLOGY

Now that the heliocentric theory has been proved to be true, theology has made its adjustments, and no one finds his religious faith disturbed by the idea that the earth revolves around the sun. The immensely grander conception of the universe and its Creator opened up to the human mind by the heliocentric doctrine is one which no one now would consent to give up. It has become so intimate a part of our customary thinking that theologians vie with astronomers in denouncing the ignorance of one who proclaims his adherence to the geocentric theory. That such a one is not today thrown into prison and persecuted for his views is due rather to our more advanced stage of civilization than to a weakening of our religious faith.

The next great conflict between science and ignorance came with the announcement of Newton's discovery of the *law of gravitation,* an application of Kepler's three laws of motion, which upon their publication had been condemned by the ecclesiastical authorities in their ignorance because these laws seemed to them to limit divine providence by the operation of natural law. While this again appears on the surface as a conflict with theology, it was in reality a conflict between ignorant theologians and supposed scientists on the one hand, in short between those bound by prejudice and tradition, and those who on the other hand because of their knowledge were in advance of their times. However, Newton wrote when the struggles of the Protestant Reformation were still occupying the time and attention of the theologians, and so, unnoticed in that age of warring ecclesiastics, Newton's sublime theory gradually established itself without subjecting its author to the penalties suffered by Galileo. Moreover, the law of gravitation requires for its proper understanding a degree of knowledge by no means widespread at that time. Its relation to current theology was therefore unappreciated except by the few, though destined eventually to have a profound influence, perhaps because perceived only by the most intelligent. That theologians to a certain etxent made the mistake of not adjusting their dogmas to accord with Newton's doctrine was, as LeConte has pointed out, the real ground of the 18th century skepticism as instanced by Voltaire and his followers. But after all the contest was between profound knowledge and ignorance. That the result of the conflict was not inimical to religion is seen in the fact that no one now appears to have his Christian faith disturbed by the theory of gravitation.

The next great conflict occurred in the realm of geology over the question of the antiquity of the earth. By *scientific methods,* Bishop Usher, in 1650, had fixed a date for the creation of the world. His method was faulty and no Biblical scholar today accepts his results. Yet in the 17th century, Lightfoot, vice-chancellor of the University of Cambridge, is said to have "declared that the Scriptures taught that 'heaven and earth, center and circumference, were created all together,

SCIENCE AND THEOLOGY

in the same instant,' and that 'this work took place and man was created by the Trinity on October 23, 4004 B.C., at nine o'clock in the morning.'"
Needless to say the Bible lends no countenance to any such conclusion as this, yet because it was apparently arrived at by logical reasoning, the multitude received it as part and parcel of their theological belief. When, therefore, geologists, like Lyell, announced their conclusion that the earth had existed throughout untold ages before the advent of man, most of the devout Christians of the period were horror-struck and were strenuously disinclined to adjust their thinking to accord with the new discoveries. The discussion on this question was often marked by bitterness and anger, but inevitably the hypothesis founded upon inaccurate calculation and inadequate knowledge of fact had to give way. Ignorance was vanquished by science until today even the most orthodox have adjusted their theological thinking to the idea of the great antiquity of the earth. Now that our eyes have been opened even he who runs may read the evidence that the geological record extends over millions of years.

The fifth conflict, that over the antiquity of man, and the sixth, that about evolution, are considered at length in later chapters of this volume. We shall anticipate the conclusions here only to say that there are many intelligent and fully informed among both scientists and theologians who find their Christian faith in no wise harmed by the scientific doctrine regarding both these questions. May it not be that the reason why many still look askance at these doctrines and fear their effect upon Christian faith and morals is that they have considered them only superficially and in connection with ill-grounded tradition, and that when seen in their true light, they will be found to be no more disastrous to Christian faith than the heliocentric theory of our universe or the law of gravitation? In the light of past experience, let us be careful how we congeal our theology around the outgrown scientific hypotheses which were developed when ignorance of the laws of nature was profound, lest unhappily we may find ourselves at last holding but the dead husks of theology in our hands while the world in general has passed us by to receive joyously the new light of truth. Let us be careful lest we be found eventually standing on the side of ignorant tradition instead of real knowledge. For be assured, ignorance can never triumph in the long run over knowledge of the truth. Whatever is true is of God and will prevail.

PART ONE

SCIENCE

CHAPTER III

THE FACT OF EVOLUTION

THE origin of the idea of the gradual development of species by descent with modification is frequently but erroneously ascribed to Darwin. While that great English naturalist did more perhaps than any other one man to secure the general acceptance of the idea by scientists, still he was by no means the first to advocate it. As far back as written history goes, men have speculated upon the method of creation. Three theories have been held, each about as old as the others. These are: first, the theory that species have always existed as they now are; second, the theory of creation by special divine fiat; and third, the theory of the gradual development of increasingly complex species from very simple beginnings.

The first of these theories is demonstrably false and has therefore had little influence on the course of human thought. The other two have been alternately or concurrently held by speculative philosophers since the days of ancient Greece, and the early Hebrew authors. The theory of special creation which during the 16th century was adopted as the orthodox teaching of the Church is one which obviously cannot be subjected to direct scientific proof or disproof. If creation took place in the miraculous manner postulated by this theory there was no man present to record his observations of the event, and like any other long past historical occurrence can only be established by the law of probability or by some other than human testimony. The third theory regards the creation as a continuous process going on today as well as in the past, and is therefore subject to demonstration or disproof by current events. It is the only one of the three which can be subjected to scientific investigation, and for this reason, if for no other, commends itself as a working hypothesis to scientists. While the demonstration of the incorrectness of the theory of evolution would not thereby logically demonstrate the correctness of the theory of special creation, nevertheless since the latter is the only other theory of creation at present in the field, the practical effect would be to establish that theory in the minds of people generally.

Before giving a *résumé* of the evidence on which scientists base their conclusion that evolution is a demonstrated fact, attention must be called to a general misapprehension among those who have not given this question special attention. This misapprehension is the common one of confusing the Darwinian theory of natural selection, or as Spencer termed it, the survival of the fittest, with the idea of evolution itself. Various attempts at an explanation of the method of evolution had been advanced before the time of Darwin, notably the Buffonian theory of the effect of changes in environmental conditions, such as climate, elevations and subsidence of the earth's crust, with concomitant expansions or contractions of the sea, etc.; secondly, the Lamarckian theory of the inherited effects of use and disuse, or more technically stated, the theory of the inheritance of bodily characteristics acquired during the lifetime of the individual animal or plant; and finally the Cuvierian theory of catastrophic extinctions of local faunas and floras followed by restocking through the immigration of new forms from elsewhere, or, as D'Orbigny suggested, by a succession of special creations. None of these hypotheses gained wide acceptance among the scientists of their day, because they were based almost wholly upon speculative considerations. Darwin's theory was based upon well established and well known facts, marshalled in numbers so great as to appeal at once to biologists, and upon perfectly logical deductions from these facts. Much of the evidence on which Darwin rested the support of his theory told weightily in favor of the underlying hypothesis of evolution and did more than anything else had done to bring about the general acceptance of that idea by his scientific colleagues. But Darwin's theory of natural selection has been found inadequate to explain all the facts and phenomena of nature to which it has been applied. Its sufficiency as an explanation has been under fire from the scientific ranks almost from the moment of its publication in 1859.

Echoes of this attack upon Darwin's explanation of the method by which evolution may have occurred have been carried over into the minds of the non-scientific public and have led to the entirely erroneous conclusion that the idea of evolution itself was under fire. The popular association of Darwin's name with the authorship of the theory of evolution has been responsible for this misunderstanding of the situation. Several theories have been advanced of late years which were intended more or less entirely to replace the Darwinian theory of natural selection as an explanation of the evolutionary process, but in every case they have been founded upon the postulate of the correctness of the evolutionary idea. Some of these, notably the De Vriesian theory of mutations, have had the merit of having been based upon the experimental method, and are therefore hypotheses that appeal to biologists in method if not in results. But it must be understood that Darwin's theory and all the others which have been advanced in explanation of the method of evolution may prove inadequate or even incorrect without in the least affecting the standing of the evolutionary idea itself.

With this situation clearly in mind it may be profitable to give a resumé of the evidence on which the doctrine of evolution rests. Only a brief outline can be given, for the literature devoted to this subject would fill a fair-sized library. The interested reader will find numerous volumes presenting the evidence in greater or less detail, among others, "The Theory of Evolution," by Dr.

THE FACT OF EVOLUTION

W. B. Scott, of Princeton University, will be found to give an excellent, but fairly brief exposition, free from technicalities. "Readings in Evolution, Heredity and Eugenics," by Dr. H. H. Newman, of the University of Chicago, is an excellent introduction to the subject, and of course no one can afford to overlook that old classic, Darwin's "Origin of Species." It would be better to begin one's reading with one or both of the more modern works cited before reading the last.

In 1758, the famous Swedish naturalist, Linnaeus, published the tenth edition of his "Systema Naturæ" in which he named and described about 4,000 species of animals, all that were known to zoologists at that time. At the present time the number of animal species that have been named and described is at least one hundred times as great, and it has been estimated that probably not half of the existing species have yet come into the hands of the systematist or classifier of animals. In the days of Linnaeus when the number of known kinds of animals and plants was comparatively small the term "species" had a definite significance. It was thought that on the day of creation a single pair of each kind had been made out of hand, and that the representatives of each species today were the lineal descendants of the original pair. Each species seemed to be a strictly circumscribed group that could be assigned to a definite pigeon-hole in a museum collection. As collections increased, however, it was soon found that hitherto supposedly distinct species had intergrades so that the more extensively were these species known the greater was the difficulty of assigning them definite limits. This difficulty was met by the supposition that species may have undergone modifications in various directions and that instead of there having been originally created a pair of each kind now existing, there had been created a pair that were the lineal ancestors not of a single but of several present-day species. Such a group of related species constitutes what biologists term a "genus"; according to this hypothesis there were originally created, not *species* in the present sense of that term, but *genera*. For example, the genus *Canis* includes all the dogs, *i.e.* wolves, coyotes, etc., as well as the various types of the domesticated dogs. It was thought that there had been originally created a single pair of dogs, but that the descendants of this original pair after their departure from the Garden of Eden had spread over the surface of the earth, and in response to the different climates and other conditions of life had varied into the species or varieties now known.

However, a wider acquaintance with the earth's fauna soon showed that even genera sometimes intergrade, or else that there are or have been (preserved as fossils) forms which could not be placed in the genera as previously understood. Similar genera are considered to constitute a *family*. Thus the dogs, wolves, foxes, jackals, etc., all *doglike*, yet differing in important generic characters, constitute the family *Canidae*. Inter-

THE FACT OF EVOLUTION

grades between the genera, however, led to the conception that probably not the genera as such, but the *family* (in this technical sense) had been represented by a single pair in the original creation. But families of animals also show certain important resemblances in structure so that they are associated in groups of a higher rank termed *orders*. Thus, the dogs, bears, weasels, cats, et al., constitute the order *Carnivora,* or the flesh-eating animals. At the present time these families are quite distinct, but in past geological times there were annectant forms which render it very difficult to separate families. The same is true in reference to the *Classes* into which the orders have been grouped, and the classes which constitute a given *Branch* of the Animal Kingdom are often more or less closely united by intergrading forms. For example it is sometimes impossible to decide whether a given fossil should be classed as a reptile or a batrachian. Even between the branches of the Animal Kingdom some clearly intergrading forms are known. Thus, there is a group of animals known as *Peripatus,* which in about half of its structural characteristics may be classed with the segmented worms, but on account of about an equal number of structural features it resembles the *Arthropods,* or the branch which includes such forms as the lobsters, crabs, spiders, and insects.

Now, applying the hypothesis of special creation to these facts, the specially created "parent" becomes in turn the ancestor not of a species merely, nor of a genus, nor family, nor order, nor class, nor even a whole branch of the Animal Kingdom, but it becomes a very primitive lowly organized creature that is ancestral to all or many of the now widely different species, which have arisen by a process of descent with modification. In short, the theory of special creation becomes indistinguishable from the theory of evolution.

The founder of the science of comparative anatomy was Cuvier, the leader of biological investigation in France during the first third of the nineteenth century. He found that in regard to structure the whole Animal Kingdom is built upon only a few (four according to Cuvier) fundamental types or plans. These he regarded as *ideal types* or concepts of the Creator, like the blueprints of an architect, but modified in detail in different species. Similarity in structure therefore meant *subjective,* not *objective,* relationship between the forms displaying it. Each organism, barring accident or disease, was supposed to have been perfectly designed for its place and function in nature. Adaptation, which is so generally apparent in the relations between organisms and their environment, was held to be the result of the *perfect* adjustment of the Creator's plan to the end in view. Intensive study of adaptation has served to make clear beyond the possibility of contradiction that *perfect adaptation* rarely, if ever, is to be found in nature. The idea that a given organ is the *best possible* for its use can be shown to be untrue in innumerable cases. Organs are adapted to their use to the extent that they

THE FACT OF EVOLUTION

enable their possessors "to get by" and usually no more. Thus, the vertebrate eye was a favorite object for discussion on this view, but the truth is that as a mechanism for receiving and recording images of the external world, it is so imperfect that were a camera maker to try to sell such an imperfect product, he would soon find himself without a market. Any eye-specialist can point out numerous ways in which the structure of the eye, wonderful as it is, might be improved to serve better its assigned function. In fact, every pair of eye-glasses bears mute testimony to this fact. The realization of these facts was a hard blow to the advocates of special creation, for it would indicate a lack of skill or foresight not to be thought of in an all-wise and all-powerful Creator.

Moreover, an examination of the structure of the corresponding organs in various animals sets the matter in a quite different light. For example, organs for locomotion may serve the functions of crawling, walking, running, swimming, climbing, flying, or burrowing. It is evident that a limb perfectly adapted for flying needs to be arranged quite differently from one adapted for burrowing or running. To be perfectly adapted for its particular function each should have its own particular structural plan. The sails of a yacht are not designed on the plan of a screw-propeller or paddle-wheel. And yet, an examination of the limbs of a turtle, a bear, a horse, a whale, a monkey, a bird, a bat, and a mole reveals the fact that these are all built on the same fundamental plan; that bone for bone, and muscle for muscle they are all essentially alike. The differences are superficial and consist in the greater development of certain parts and the less development of other parts. Moreover, each of these limbs has exactly the same origin in the embryo, and in the fossil remains of their annectant species these limbs can frequently be seen to grade into a common primitive type. These similarities in origin and structure of corresponding organs are indicative of *homology,* that is they mean descent with modification in adaptation to different uses; in short, they indicate genetic relationship. On the basis of special creation they have no meaning or else seem to limit the exercise of creative power.

But still more suggestive is the presence in all animals of a greater or less number (over 200 in man) of vestigial structures which in related species are often well developed and of functional importance. This fact has no meaning on the hypothesis of special creation, while on the hypothesis of descent with modification it finds a satisfactory explanation on the ground that these are organs once well developed and useful to the ancestors of the species in which they now occur only as useless or even harmful vestiges. That they are not always merely useless, in which case they often require an unnecessary expenditure of energy for their maintenance, but are sometimes harmful even to the extent of being the seat of fatal maladies, may be recognized in the familiar example of the vermiform appendix in man. The

THE FACT OF EVOLUTION

fact that certain snakes have recognizable vestiges of limbs can only mean that these animals have descended from ancestors which possessed locomotor appendages; the presence of vestigial incisor teeth in the upper jaw of the embryo calf, or of teeth in both jaws of the embryo parrot, can only be an indication that the ancestors of our cattle had upper incisors and the ancestors of modern parrots were toothed. In fact, toothed birds occur as fossils in the Cretaceous deposits of Kansas and in the Jurassic of Germany. The clearly developed third eye on the top of the head of a New Zealand lizard (*Sphenodon*) indicates that certain vestigial structures on the roof of the brain in other reptiles, birds and mammals, are the vestiges of organs of sight. That these vestiges occur in all these classes of vertebrates argues for a common though distant ancestry.

A study of the embryological development of animals reveals a large series of facts hard to explain on the basis of special creation, but clearly what would be expected if descent with modification has occurred. Thus, in the development of the mammalian heart, one finds it at an early stage in the form of a simple straight tube, suggestive of the heart in that most primitive vertebrate, *Amphioxus*. By the process of elongation and twisting, accompanied by unequal growth in various regions, this simple tube becomes converted into a two-chambered heart in all respects similar in plan and relationships to the two-chambered heart of the fish. By the formation of septa, or walls, these two chambers, an auricle and a ventricle, are divided, first into three chambers, two auricles and a ventricle, recalling the heart of a frog or reptile, and then into four chambers, characteristic of the bird or mammal.

Leading away from the two-chambered heart of the embryo of a reptile, bird or mammal, there is a series of paired blood vessels, *aortic arches,* which pass dorsalward in the side walls of the neck between a series of openings identical in manner of formation, location and arrangement with the gill-slits in the embryo fish. The aortic arches, six pairs in number, undergo certain modifications in the course of embryonic development by which they become converted into the gill vessels of the fishes; into three pairs of arches in the frog; a single pair in the reptiles; and finally into a single unpaired vessel in birds and mammals. But in the last mentioned cases, the arch on the right side persists in the bird, while it is the one on the left that remains in mammals. On the hypothesis of special creation this very complex history of the aorta is unintelligible, while on the hypothesis of descent with modification it is quite in accord with the idea that the ancestral forms of the higher animals passed through a stage in which they breathed by means of gills. In fact, in the case of the frog, that very thing happens to this day in individual development, since in the tadpole there are gills and gill-slits supplied with aortic arches, which at the metamorphosis become transformed into the arrangement found in the adult frog.

THE FACT OF EVOLUTION

The brain, the respiratory organs, the excretory system, the reproductive system, in fact all organ systems of the vertebrate tell the same story. But we have sketched only a late chapter in the history. The earlier chapters are just as illuminating. Every multicellular organism begins its individual existence as a single unit of structure called a cell. This cell is in its essential structures identical with the simplest one-celled animals (*Protozoa*). By the process of cell-division, this egg-cell, in which the multicellular animal starts its development, becomes converted into a spherical body structurally resembling a colonial protozoan, such as *Volvox*. By a process of folding in on one side this sphere (*blastula*) becomes converted into a two-layered sack (*gastrula*) essentially like the adult form of *Microhydra,* a little freshwater relative of the corals and jellyfishes. From this point on, the different branches of the animal kingdom diverge in the course of their development, though here and there stages are found that seem to indicate a closer relationship between some of them than exists between these and other branches. Thus among an interesting group of very small animals, called *Rotifers* because they appear to have wheels on their heads, there is a genus named *Trochosphaera,* which, when adult, very closely resembles a larval form found in many worms and molluscs. The larva of the segmented worms has some resemblances to the very young embryonic stages of the vertebrates.

This parallelism in development among the embryos of many species, so well marked among the vertebrates, was long ago pointed out by Agassiz, who however apparently did not realize its force as an argument for descent with modification. Often these resemblances are not merely general but pertain to relatively unimportant details. The wing of the bird, for example, at one stage, cannot be distinguished from the fore-limb of a cat; in fact, in the chick "the hand is represented in the embryo of six days (incubation) by the spatulate extremity of the fore-limb, which includes the elements of the carpus (wrist), metacarpus (palm), and phalanges (fingers). From this expansion five digital (finger) rays grow out simultaneously, the first (thumb) and fifth (little finger) being relatively small; the second, third, and fourth represent the persistent digits.... Thus there are distinct indications of a pentadactyl (five-fingered) stage in the development of the bird's wing." (F. R. Lillie, "The Development of the Chick," p. 436.) One needs only to examine the next chicken wing served on his table to understand how greatly this fundamental five-fingered plan is modified in the adult. The facts can mean only that the ancestors of modern birds were at one time possessed of five-fingered hands.

But the line of evidence which perhaps more than any other was convincing to Darwin and his contemporaries was that derived from the geological record. This is now much more completely known than it was fifty years ago and every new expedition sent out in search of fossils but piles

THE FACT OF EVOLUTION

up the evidence for the derivation of species by descent with modification. This evidence is of two sorts: *general* and *special*.

The general evidence is found in the fact that the oldest strata composing the earth's crust, in which there is any evidence of life, indicate the existence only of the very simplest unicellular plants. The earliest known animal fossils comprise only unicellular forms; successively more recent strata contain the fossil remains at first of the most generalized sorts of invertebrates, such as sponges, jellyfishes and worms; then by the Cambrian times—the earliest fossiliferous rocks known to Darwin—practically all the chief invertebrate branches were represented by primitive forms which gave place in later periods to the more highly specialized members of the same groups. The branch of the vertebrates, or backboned animals, was the last to make its appearance, in the form, so far as it is now known, of primitive fishes. Lung-fishes and batrachians came in later; still later the reptiles arrived as aquatic forms so primitive as to be distinguished from the batrachians sometimes only with difficulty by the expert. During the Mesozoic age the reptiles diverged in many directions and became adapted to life on land as well as in the water, some becoming huge and bizarre in appearance, while others acquired the power of flight. In the Triassic the first mammals made their appearance, small primitive, presumably egg-laying creatures displaying numerous structural resemblances to some of the reptiles. As the reptiles decreased in importance the mammals advanced to replace them, displaying divergent adaptations to all possible modes of life, some flying, some swift-footed and cursorial, others heavy limbed and slow of foot. The egg-laying mammals, for the most part, gave place to those which bring forth their young alive. In the Jurassic the first known birds appeared, but still so reptilian with their teeth, long many-vertebrated tail, and weakly developed wings with three *free* fingers, that were it not for their feathers they might readily be mistaken for reptiles. The Cretaceous birds were still toothed, though diversified both as aquatic and as land-living species. All of these facts speak so conclusively against the traditional view of creation and so clearly in favor of a progressive development that it is not surprising that if the evolutionary hypothesis had not already been advanced, paleontologists would have been driven to its formulation on the basis of their discoveries alone.

The special evidence from the geological record is found in the more detailed history of certain family groups, like that of the camels, the elephants, or the horses. Despite the fact that opponents of the evolutionary theory have dubbed the pedigree of the horse "evolution's hobby-horse," the fact remains that the history of the evolution of this familiar animal is so extensively and so completely known that it illustrates perhaps more clearly than any other case that may be cited the type of facts needed to set forth this special line

THE FACT OF EVOLUTION

of evidence. Briefly and only in outline this history is as follows:

The horse originated in North America in Eocene times, with *Eohippus,* a graceful little creature about a foot high at the withers, with arched back, short head and neck, with limbs of moderate length bearing four complete toes on the front foot, and three on the hind foot, though with a small remnant of the fourth and, in at least one specimen, a tiny vestige of the fifth toe is also present. *Orohippus* exhibits an advance in the loss of even the remnant of the fourth toe, in the shortening of the outer finger of the hand, besides the development of certain complexities in its molar teeth. It was thirteen and one-half inches high. In the Upper Eocene, *Epihippus* occurred, somewhat larger than *Orohippus,* still with four fingers and three toes on each hand and foot respectively, but the weight was borne more on the middle fingers and toes, which were slightly larger than the others. In the Oligocene we find first *Mesohippus,* about the size of a coyote, with only three functional digits on each foot, though the middle one in every case was much larger than the lateral ones and bore much more of the creature's weight. Several species are known, of which *Mesohippus bairdi* was about eighteen inches high, while *Mesohippus intermedius* reached a height of two feet. The teeth were more complex than in the preceding forms. *Mesohippus* of the Lower and Middle Oligocene was replaced by *Miohippus* of the Upper Oligocene. In the Miocene,

Hypohippus attained a height of forty inches, with three-toed feet in which the middle toes were much the largest. *Merychippus,* though still three-toed, had the middle toes so much developed that the lateral ones never touched the ground; its milk teeth were short crowned and had little or no cement, like the permanent teeth of its predecessors, but its permanent teeth were long-crowned and fully cemented, forming a transition to the condition of the teeth in more modern horses. In the Upper Miocene and Pliocene occurred *Protohippus* in which both the milk teeth and the permanent teeth were moderately long-crowned and cemented, though the feet were still three-toed. *Pliohippus* was a stockier animal, about ten hands high, with more nearly the build of modern horses, and with the toes reduced to only one on each foot. It was the first one-toed horse. The modern horse, *Equus,* first appeared in the Upper Pliocene and represents the culmination of the line. Some species in the Pleistocene attained a height of about fifteen hands and had somewhat the proportions of a western broncho. At the present time there is but one species of true wild horse, the Prejvalski horse or tarpan of central Asia, though at least three other types of true horses are represented among our domesticated breeds. Near the true horses, but specifically distinct from them, are the the kiang of Mongolia and Turkestan, the zebras of Africa, and the ass, a native of Africa but domesticated and distributed well over the earth.

THE FACT OF EVOLUTION

This brief outline is perhaps enough to indicate how complete is the geological history of the development of this well known animal from more primitive ancestors. Each step in the history illustrated by the succession of forms mentioned, corresponds exactly with the succession of geological strata from the oldest Eocene to the present. One can hardly look upon the splendid display of these fossil horses in the American Museum of Natural History, in New York, or at Yale and elsewhere, without being convinced that he has spread out before his eyes the veritable story of the evolutionary development of these animals through the millions of years which elapsed between *Eohippus* and the modern *Equus caballus*. Every link in the chain is strong evidence of the truth of the evolutionary hypothesis; there is not a shadow of evidence anywhere in the whole series in favor of the hypothesis of special creation. Did this case stand alone, the evidence would be very strong, but when one considers that this same sort of evidence is furnished by several other families of mammals, by reptiles, and fishes, by the nautiloids among the molluscs, and other invertebrates, the significance seems overwhelming.

The evidence in favor of the evolutionary hypothesis derived from a consideration of the geographical distribution of animals and plants is in its way also quite convincing. Only a few of the facts can be set forth here, though the interested reader will find several volumes devoted to the subject by Wallace, Beddard, Gadow, and other well-known and capable zoologists. It was observations in this field which perhaps more than any other first converted Darwin from a belief in special creation to an advocacy of the evolutionary hypothesis. A few paragraphs selected from the "Origin of Species" (p. 360) will set forth the facts in summary form:

"If the difficulties be not insuperable in admitting that in the long course of time all the individuals of the same species, and likewise of the several species belonging to the same genus, have proceeded from some one source; then all the grand leading facts of geographical distribution are explicable on the theory of migration, together with subsequent modification and the multiplication of new forms. We can thus understand the high importance of barriers, whether of land or water, in not only separating, but in apparently forming the several zoological and botanical provinces. We can thus understand the concentration of related species within the same areas, and how it is that under different latitudes, for instance in South America, the inhabitants of the plains and mountains, of the forests, marshes, and deserts, are linked together in so mysterious a manner, and likewise linked to the extinct beings which formerly inhabited the same continent. Bearing in mind that the mutual relation of organism to organism is of the highest importance, we can see why two areas having nearly the same physical conditions should often be inhabited by very different forms of life; for according to the length of

THE FACT OF EVOLUTION

time which has elapsed since the colonists entered one of the regions, or both; according to the nature of the communication which allowed certain forms and not others to enter, either in greater or lesser numbers; according or not, as those which entered happened to come into more or less direct competition with each other and with the aborigines; and according as the immigrants were capable of varying more or less rapidly, there would ensue in the two or more regions, independently of their physical conditions, infinitely diversified conditions of life,—and there would be an almost endless amount of organic action and reaction,—and we should find some groups of beings greatly, and some only slightly modified,—some developed in great force, some existing in scanty numbers—and this we do find in the several great geographical provinces of the world.

"On these same principles we can understand, as I have endeavored to show, why oceanic islands should have few inhabitants, but that of these, a large proportion should be endemic or peculiar; and why, in relation to the means of migration, one group of beings should have all its species peculiar, and another group, even within the same class, should have all its species the same with those in an adjoining quarter of the world. We can see why whole groups of organisms, as batrachians and terrestrial mammals, should be absent from oceanic islands, whilst the most isolated islands should possess their own peculiar species of aerial mammals or bats. We can see why in islands there should be some relation between the presence of mammals, in a more or less modified condition, and the depth of the sea between such islands and the mainland. We can clearly see why all the inhabitants of an archipelago, though specifically distinct on the several islets, should be closely related to each other; and should likewise be related, but less closely, to those of the nearest continent, or other source whence immigrants might have been derived. We can see why, if there exist very closely allied or representative species in two areas, however distant from each other, some identical species will almost always there be found. . . .

"There is a striking parallelism in the laws of life throughout time and space; the laws governing the succession of forms in past times being nearly the same with those governing at the present time the differences in different areas. We see this in many facts. The endurance of each species and group of species is continuous in time; . . . so in space, it certainly is the general rule that the area inhabited by a single species, or by a group of species, is continuous, and the exceptions, which are not rare, may, as I have attempted to show, be accounted for by the former migrations under different circumstances, or through occasional means of transport, or by the species having become extinct in the intermediate tracts. Both in time and space, species and groups of species have their points of maximum development. Groups of species, living during the same period of time, or living within the same area, are often characterized by trifling features in common, as of sculpture or color. In looking to the long succession of past ages, as in looking to distant provinces throughout the world, we find that species in certain classes differ little from each other, whilst those in another class, or only in a different section of the same order, differ greatly from each other. In both time and space the lowly organized members of each class generally change less than the highly organized; but there are in both cases marked exceptions to the rule. According to our theory, these several relations throughout time and space are intelligible; for whether we look to the allied forms of life which have changed during successive ages, or to those which have changed after having migrated into distant quarters, in both cases they are connected by the same bond of ordinary generation; in both cases the laws of variation have been the same, and modifications have been accumulated by the same means. . . ."

For many centuries man was engaged in the domestication of various wild species of animals and plants. At first this process was doubtless more or less without thought or foresight, quite accidental as it were. Later man consciously selected such variations as he for any reason fancied among those which appeared from time to time in the already domesticated forms and still later he manipulated his products experimentally in order to bring about desired improvements. To such an extent has this been done that it is rarely possible at this time to determine exactly what wild species was the original progenitor of the domesticated forms. This modification by man has sometimes resulted in the production of several forms from one original source as is shown in the cabbage, where starting with the common wild cabbage of the Mediterranean shore, there have been produced such widely different things as the various kinds of cultivated cabbage, the cauliflower, also in several varieties, the broccoli, the kohl-rabi of at least three distinct sorts, the brussels sprouts, kale, and perhaps others. The Indian love-apple has been developed almost within the memory of people still living into the manifold varieties of the cultivated tomato, some of which are so well marked and breed so true to type that no botanist finding them in a state of nature would hesitate to call them distinct species. Dogs, cats, horses, cattle, sheep, hogs, chickens, turkeys, ducks, and geese, all these and others, but exemplify the same condition. For many years horticulturalists and animal breeders did not realize what they were really doing, but now that the better informed of them understand that they are engaged in the evolution of the forms with which they are dealing, the laws of variation and heredity are being consciously applied. Hence a Burbank can in a few years produce almost any variety he desires, even to the production of Indian corn or maize from the teosinte of our southern hay-fields.

Taking the hint from the production of varieties of cultivated plants or domesticated animals, students of evolution have for the past twenty

THE FACT OF EVOLUTION

years, largely under the influence of the Dutch botanist, De Vries, definitely undertaken the experimental production of new species. The results are so numerous and so conclusive that it is no exaggeration to say that now we have seen literally hundreds of new species produced by experiment either in laboratory or field. It is no longer possible to assert with truth that no man has seen one species changed into another. *This is evolution;* there is involved no hypothesis or theory, in the ordinary acceptation of those terms. It is *the demonstration of a fact* which can no longer be successfully gainsaid.

A somewhat different line of experiment has within the past few years most unexpectedly supplied evidence for the evolutionary hypothesis of a most convincing sort. This is the work of Dr. George H. F. Nuttall, of the University of Cambridge, on "Blood Immunity and Blood Relationship," published in 1904, and that of Professors Reichert and Brown, of the University of Pennsylvania, published in 1909, on "The Differentiation and Specificity of Corresponding Proteins and Other Vital Substances in Relation to Biological Classification and Organic Evolution."

Nuttall's technique and results are as follows: A rabbit is given introperitoneal injections of 5-10 cc. of defibrinated human blood twice weekly for about six weeks, then bled a week after the last injection, and the clear serum separated from the clotted blood. We thus obtain a reagent which when added to clear human blood serum immediately gives a copious white precipitate. If the rabbit serum be diluted 1:50 or 1:100 as a standard, so that it shall always be present in uniform quantity in all the tests made, and the serums to be tested for blood relationship given various dilutions—1:100, 1:1,000, 1:10,000, 1:100,000, etc.—and the mixtures of the test (rabbit) serum and the serum to be tested allowed to stand for, say, thirty minutes as a fixed period, it will be found that the reaction of precipitation is specific in that closely related bloods precipitate in greater dilution and in larger quantity than bloods more distantly related. Thus, human serum may be precipitated with anti-human (rabbit) serum in dilutions even reaching 1:100,000; the blood of anthropoid (manlike) apes in slightly less dilutions; those of other apes in decidedly less dilutions; those of lower monkeys in less and less dilution the further they are zoologically removed from man; those of lower mammals only in the concentrated form, if at all; and the bloods of still lower vertebrates and invertebrates not at all.[1]

Professor William B. Scott, of Princeton University ("The Theory of Evolution," p. 78) notes that "anti-pig serum gives maximum reactions only with the bloods of other species of the same family, moderate reactions with those of ruminants and camels, and moderate or slight reactions with those of whales. Anti-llama serum gives a moderate reaction with the blood of the camel,

[1] Slightly modified from the account given by McFarland, in his "Biology, General and Medical."

and the close relationship between the deer-family and the great host of antelopes, sheep, goats and oxen is clearly demonstrated. Strong anti-turtle serum gives maximum reactions only with the bloods of turtles and crocodiles, with those of lizards and snakes the results are almost negative. With the egg-albumins of reptiles and birds a moderate reaction is given.

"These experiments indicate that there is a close relationship between lizards and snakes, on the one hand, and turtles and crocodiles, on the other. They further indicate that birds are more nearly allied with the turtle-crocodile series than with the lizard-snake series, results for which paleontological studies had already prepared us."

The work of Reichert and Brown had to do with the oxy-hemoglobin crystals of the blood. According to them, "it has been conclusively shown not only that corresponding hemoglobins are not identical, but also that their peculiarities are of a positive generic specificity. . . . Moreover, it has been found that one can with some certainty predict by these peculiarities, without previous knowledge of the species from which the hemoglobins were derived, whether or not interbreeding is probable or possible, and also certain characteristics of habit, etc. . . . No difficulty was experienced in forecasting similarities and dissimilarities of habit in *Sciuridae* (squirrels), *Muridae* (mice and rats), *Felidae* (cats), etc., not because it is *per se* the determining factor, but because . . . it serves as an index (gross though it be, with our present very limited knowledge) of those physico-chemical properties which serve directly or indirectly to differentiate genera, species, and individuals."

But the clinching argument for the experienced biologist has not yet been mentioned. It is the fact that he is constantly brought into contact with phenomena, oftentimes of little importance in themselves, all of which seem to point in the same direction, *i.e.,* toward the evolutionary hypothesis. It is the cumulative effect of these little things which finally decides the matter for him. For example, some years ago the author was engaged in a study of the development of the eggs in the Cuban blind-fishes. These interesting fishes, two genera of them, are not only blind, but they are the only freshwater representatives of a family of fishes the other members (genera) of which live in the sea. Moreover, they do not lay their eggs, as ordinary fishes do, but bring forth their young alive. These young, two to fifteen in a season, are fully formed and large in size, being at birth sometimes nearly one-third the length of the mother and have well developed eyes. This suggests at once that the ancestors of these fishes had sight like ordinary species today. But in studying the development of their eggs, it was found that these arise within the ovaries of the mother fish in groups of hundreds or even thousands each. Moreover, each ovary usually contains a dozen or more of these "nests" of young eggs, so that at least a hundred thousand young eggs begin to develop in each female. Yet very soon in the course

THE FACT OF EVOLUTION

of this process *one* egg, and usually only one, in each "nest" begins to forge ahead of the others, soon far outstripping them in size, and then, to cap the climax, this precocious egg literally proceeds to eat up all the other eggs in its own "nest!" The final result is the birth of only a few young, alive and far on their road to maturity, instead of the early deposition of hundreds or thousands of eggs as in the case of more familiar species.

Now, such facts as these have but one plausible explanation. These blind, viviparous, fresh-water Cuban fishes must have descended with modification from seeing, egg-laying, marine forms. In other words, the species as found today must have been produced by a process of evolution from an ancestral form quite different from them in structure, mode of life, and manner of reproduction. Evolution is the only satisfactory answer to the questions raised by these phenomena. Such observations are far from uncommon; in fact, they occur with such frequency in the experience of every biologist, that the fact of evolution becomes an inescapable conclusion. Hence practically every biologist who has made any important investigations in his field is a convinced evolutionist.

CHAPTER IV

HAS MAN EVOLVED?

THERE are those who are willing to admit the possibility of, or even to accept, the evolutionary hypothesis when applied to plants and the "lower" animals, who nevertheless, for one reason or another, reject its application to man. It becomes necessary, therefore, to consider as briefly, but as fairly as possible, the evidence of man's ascent from lowlier forms. The question whether, if one admits the evolution of man's bodily structures, his mind or soul may not have had a special origin, will be reserved for a later chapter.

The evidence relied upon to show that the human species has had an evolutionary history is the same in kind as that set forth in the preceding chapter for evolution in general. Thus the human species is not a homogeneous one, but is composed of several well marked varieties, so distinct that there is little doubt but that in any other form than man they would be ranked as legitimate species. In fact some anthropologists have so regarded them. These varieties or races, moreover, comprise literally hundreds of sub-varieties, each distinguished by a definite combination of physical characteristics. On the basis of the origin of man by special creation it cannot be denied that the species has undergone a most remarkable amount of variation. The opponent of the doctrine of evolution admits this, but falls back upon the argument that these races are not true species because they are fertile *inter se*. It has long been maintained that the surest mark of true species is their inability to hybridize, or if hybrid offspring are produced, that the latter are sterile. As one extreme opponent has strikingly expressed the idea: "The stubborn mule still blocks the way of evolution."

That many or even most true species in nature are sterile *inter se* may be true, but the fact remains that there are many which are not. There are two well marked species of Old World camels, the African dromedary, or one-humped camel, and the Asiatic or Bactrian camel with two humps, which despite their distinctness have bred together. In South America, the llama has been bred with the very distinct alpaca and the offspring are fertile. Among the deer several species are known to interbreed; while among the Bovidæ, or cattle in the broadest sense, the zebu (*Bos indicus*), or sacred humped ox of India, has been crossed with the gayal (*Bibos frontalis*), a true buffalo. The female offspring of such a cross has even been mated with the American bison (*Bison americanus*) and produced fertile progeny. Here are involved, not only three distinct *species,* but even three distinct *genera.* Several species of our native birds hybridize readily in a state of nature, for example, the two species of flicker, *Colaptes auratus* or yellow shafted woodpecker, and *Colaptes cafer* or red shafted woodpecker. Some years ago the author instructed his taxidermist to collect a number of flickers for mounting in a group. The first dozen specimens secured were all hybrids and showed almost a dozen degrees of intermediate conditions between the two species.

It is also well known that when the American bison is crossed with the domestic cow, the offspring are fertile if of the *female* sex, but sterile if *male*. If sterility is to be regarded as a criterion of specific distinctness, and fertility as a mark of "mere varieties," are we therefore to conclude in this case (which is by no means unique) that domestic cattle and the bison are merely varieties in the *female line,* but distinct species in the *male?* Two species of toads are known in the case of which the male of one is fertile only with females of its own species, while the male of the other is fertile with both. Do these males belong to two distinct species, while the females constitute merely two varieties? Such conclusions are such obvious absurdities that they may be left to call forth their own answers. The truth is that sterility is not always a condition that obtains between true species and fertility between mere varieties.

So one is not justified in asserting that man constitutes only a single species merely on the ground that the various so-called races are interfertile. Moreover, the degree of fertility among these races varies greatly in different cases.

Evolution and Christian Faith

But for our purpose it matters little whether man be considered as constituting one species with many varieties, or several; the fact remains that these different forms are remarkably constant when prevented from intercrossing, and that they could only have arisen by descent with modification from a common source of mankind.

The study of comparative anatomy shows that man has exactly the same kind of structural resemblances to lower forms that the latter display to one another. The skeleton of man and that of an anthropoid ape, such as the gorilla, chimpanzee, or orang-utan, is bone for bone the same. The differences are such as relate to the peculiar adaptations of each species. Thus man is a ground-living form, while these apes are adapted to live in trees. So while the foot of man has the same bones and muscles, the same nerves and blood-vessels as has their foot, it is modified in the latter case by such minor characters as the setting of the big toe at an angle to the others in order that it may be opposed to them and thus be a more skilful organ for climbing. In man, the big toe lies close to and parallel to the other toes, and moreover is so placed that the principal axis of the foot passes through it. This is an adaptation to terrestrial locomotion in which man excels all the apes. If it be objected that the gorilla and chimpanzee have thirteen pairs of ribs, while man has only twelve, it may be answered that the orang also has but twelve, while in man it is not unusual to find thirteen pairs present in cadavers dissected in ana-

HAS MAN EVOLVED?

tomical laboratories. And so the story may be indefinitely prolonged. The teeth, the head, the upper extremities, the viscera, all tell the same thing. The greatest differences lie in the size of the brain, but here the distinction is one apparently of degree, for the same structural parts are found in all. Thus as to the convolutions, the brains of apes exhibit every stage of progress, from the almost smooth brain of the marmoset to the orang and the chimpanzee, which fall but little below man. And it is most remarkable that, as soon as all the principal furrows appear, the pattern according to which they are arranged is identical with that of the corresponding furrows on the brain of man. The surface of the brain of a monkey exhibits a sort of skeleton map of man's and in the manlike apes the details become more and more filled in, until it is only in minor characters, such as the greater excavation of the anterior lobes, the constant presence of fissures usually absent in man, and the different disposition and proportions of some convolutions, that the chimpanzee's or the orang's brain can be structurally distinguished from man's. So far as cerebral structure goes, therefore, it is clear that man differs less from the chimpanzee or the orang than these do even from the monkeys, and that the differences between the brains of the chimpanzee and of man are almost insignificant, when compared with those between the chimpanzee brain and that of a lemur, among the lowest of the Primates.

It must not be overlooked, however, that there

is a very striking difference in the absolute mass and weight between the lowest adult human brain and that of the highest ape—a difference which is all the more remarkable when we recollect that a full-grown gorilla is nearly twice as heavy as the average man. It may be doubted whether a healthy human adult brain ever weighs less than 31 ounces, or that the heaviest gorilla brain exceeds 20 ounces. This is a very noteworthy circumstance, but it has little classificatory value for the simple reason that the difference in weight of brain between the highest and lowest men is far greater, both relatively and absolutely than that between the lowest man and the highest ape. The latter is represented by only about 11 ounces of cerebral matter absolutely, or by 31:20 relatively; while the former is represented by 34 ounces absolutely, or by 65:31 relatively. Whatever system of organs be studied, the comparison of their modifications in the ape series leads to one and the same result—that the structural differences which separate man from the highest apes are not so great as those which separate the latter from the lower apes. These are facts that cannot be disputed.

But if man be separated by no greater structural barrier from the "lower" animals than they are from one another—then it would seem to follow that if any process of physical causation can be discovered by which the species, genera, and families of ordinary animals have been produced, that process of causation must be sufficient to ac-

HAS MAN EVOLVED?

count for the origin of man. In other words, if the marmosets have arisen by gradual modification of the ordinary American monkeys, or if both these groups are modified ramifications of a primitive stock—then, there can be no reasonable ground for doubting that man originated either by the gradual modification of a man-like ape, or as a branch of the same primitive stock as those apes.[1]

Embryology adds its testimony in corroboration of this view, revealing that the human embryo passes through stages exactly comparable to those exhibited by the embryos of lower forms. Thus at one stage the human embryo has gill-slits and aortic arches, not to speak of a cartilaginous framework, in the sides of its neck like those of a fish; its skeletal framework is at first like that of the lancelet (*amphioxus*)—lower than any familiar type of fish—then fishlike, then decidedly reptilian, then gradually step by step it parallels the other mammals until finally it emerges as a primate, and only at last becomes distinctly human. That at one time the human embryo has a well-marked tail and later the fetus is entirely covered with hair save on the palms of the hands and the soles of the feet, are facts familiar to students of human embryology. In a very early stage the waste products of the human embryo are taken care of by a primitive sort of "kidney" (*pronephros*)

---

[1] The last three paragraphs are slightly modified from Huxley's account in his "Man's Place in Nature."

located in the neck region; later this is replaced by a second "kidney" (*mesonephros*), much more extensive in size and more complex in structure; and finally, the true kidney (*metanephros*) replaces the second and continues to function throughout life, the first two disappearing altogether except for certain vestiges connected with the reproductive system, which have no excretory function. It is suggestive that the excretory apparatus of the lancelet and lampreys consists throughout life only of the pronephros; in the fishes the mesonephros also is developed, and both it and the pronephros are functional in the adult. In the Batrachians, the pronephros degenerates and only the mesonephros persists. In the reptiles, birds, and mammals, as in man, the pronephros and mesonephros are transitory embryonic organs, replaced by the true kidneys (*metanephroi*) which function throughout life.

That the structure of the entire human embryo very closely resembles that of other mammalian embryos is well exemplified by experiences common to many instructors in the subject, who have substituted sections of pig, rabbit, cat or rat embryos in the laboratory for sections of human embryos of corresponding stages of development without the students being aware of the exchange! Moreover, even an experienced embryologist dare not preserve a series of mammalian embryos without carefully labelling each at the time it is secured, for it is almost impossible to determine whether a given specimen is human, or pig, or cat,

HAS MAN EVOLVED?

or rat, if the labels be misplaced even on specimens fairly well advanced in development. It is hard to see how such a close similarity can be accounted for except on the hypothesis of common descent.

Physiologically man's closer resemblance to the higher apes was mentioned in connection with the account of Nuttall's investigation with the serum test as described in the preceding chapter. The fact that the human tissues are chemically more like those of the anthropoids and less and less like those of other mammals the farther removed the latter are from man zoologically, amounts almost to a demonstration that man must be included in the evolutionary process. A somewhat related line of evidence is to be found in the fact that the diseases of man are shared with the apes, and even more striking is the fact that the external parasites (lice) of man are specifically and generically more closely allied to those of the anthropoids than they are to those of the lower mammals. In short, the familiar "cootie" tells the tale of man's animal derivation.

The yet few but increasingly common human fossils, as the next chapter will relate at some length, clearly tell of man's gradual development through the last half million years from a form with scant brain capacity to that of the large-brained creature of today. Some of these fossils are so clearly intermediate between man and the higher apes that it cannot even now be definitely decided whether they should be classed in the human family or with the simians; still others, while human, are clearly generically distinct from the genus *Homo*.

These being, in outline, the facts in the case, it is clear that the evolutionary hypothesis applies to man just as cogently as to the lower animals and plants. Unless one is prepared to reject the evidence *in toto,* for the latter as well as for man, there is no escape from this conclusion. One must either deny the force of the argument altogether and refuse to accept the doctrine of evolution at all, or else, if convinced that the facts reveal the evolutionary history of the lower animals, one is logically compelled to accept them for man also, if one is not to commit mental suicide.

This is not to deny that, in spite of this close similarity to the animal in his physical make-up, man stands far above all other organisms in his mental attainments. This is the ground on which the strongest arguments are based in favor of the view that man is *sui generis*—a unique production with no true kinship to the forms below him in the animal scale.

Only an elementary knowledge of biology is necessary to show, upon careful analysis, that the plants are characterized by their *simple energy-combining powers*. The green plant works with such elementary substances as water, carbon dioxide and oxygen from the air, and nitrates from the soil, which, by means of energy derived directly from the sun's rays, it combines into more complex, yet relatively simple, compounds such as the starches and sugars, fats and proteins, which serve the plant directly as food out of which it manufactures its *living substance,* the protoplasm of its cells.

The animals are not capable of thus utilizing the simple inorganic chemical compounds but must have the sugars and starches, fats and proteins already elaborated by the plants. But in addition to this distinction, the lower animals possess a positive characteristic which sets them off as beings of a higher order than the plants, namely their *space-traversing power.* Plants in general are anchored to one spot; they are dependent upon the contents of their immediate environment—upon the soil in which they are rooted, upon the atmosphere surrounding their tops, upon the supply of moisture, heat and light that chance conditions may supply to them. If food of any kind fails in one locality, the plant suffers or dies, while the animal may migrate to another region, more or less remote, where the desired food may be obtained. This *space-traversing power* of the animal is of immense importance in the maintenance of the species and, if the doctrine of evolution be accepted, accounts in a large measure for the higher organization of the animal, an organization involving the development of a central nervous system. The lowest of the animals in which the nervous system is least developed display the least of this space-traversing power and live little above the plant plane. As one ascends higher in the animal scale, the increasing development of the nervous system is correlated with increasing power of space-traversion, until it reaches its culmination in the highest animals.

Turning to man from this point of view, one finds that in common with the lower animals he is a space-traversing organism, and like them he is dependent upon the lower organisms for his food. But no other animal has the space-traversing power so well developed as he, consequently no other animal has so wide a distribution over the earth, no other animal can make its home in so many different types of environment, except some few domesticated forms which are dependent upon man for their existence. Man lives from the equator almost to the poles, where variations in temperature are extreme; he lives on the islands of the sea no less than upon the continents; fertile plain and desert, valley and mountain top, all have been brought into his service. This extreme *power of space-traversion* is correlated with the high development of his central nervous system.

But while man here again reveals his relationship to the lower animals, nevertheless he is characterized by the possession of a power that raises him almost infinitely above even those animals that stand nearest to him. He is characterized by the *time-relating power* which he shares with no other form. Man not only has had a history, but *he knows it*. He is aware not merely of present conditions, but is capable of forming and retaining concepts of past conditions. Furthermore, relating the past experiences of the race with those of the present, he is more or less able to project

HAS MAN EVOLVED?

himself into the future and to foresee the consequences of present action and present conditions. It is this power that, more than anything else, marks him off from the rest of creation and leads some to accord him a special kingdom of his own.

For those who have not given special study to the question it may be difficult to understand how such a vast difference in the intellectual powers of man and the apes could fail to be associated with vast structural differences in the respective brains. The failure to discover any such marked structural differences has been used as an argument, not that they do not exist, but rather that man is incompetent to discover them. There is a fallacy in this reasoning as Huxley long ago pointed out, when he said that the validity of such an argument "hangs upon the assumption that intellectual power depends altogether on the brain—whereas the brain is only one condition out of many on which intellectual manifestations depend; the others being, chiefly, the organs of the senses and the motor apparatuses, especially those which are concerned in prehension and in the production of articulate speech. A man born dumb, notwithstanding his great cerebral mass and his inheritance of strong intellectual instincts, would be capable of few higher intellectual manifestations than an orang or a chimpanzee, if he were confined to the society of dumb associates. And yet there might not be the slightest discernible difference between his brain and that of a highly intelligent and cultivated person. The dumbness might be the result of a defective structure of the mouth, or of the tongue, or a mere defective innervation of these parts; or it might result from congenital deafness, caused by some minute defect of the internal ear, which only a careful anatomist could discover.

"The argument, that because there is an immense difference between a man's intelligence and an ape's therefore there must be an equally immense difference between their brains, appears to me to be about as well based as the reasoning by which one should endeavor to prove that, because there is a "great gulf" between a watch that keeps accurate time and another that will not go at all, there is therefore a great structural hiatus between the two watches. A hair in the balance-wheel, a little rust on the pinion, a bend in a tooth of the escapement, a something so slight that only the practised eye of the watchmaker can discover it, may be the source of all the difference. . . . Some equally inconspicuous structural difference may have been the primary cause of the immeasurable and practically infinite divergence of the human from the simian stirps." ("Man's Relations to the Lower Animals," by T. H. Huxley.)

CHAPTER V

THE GEOLOGICAL HISTORY OF MAN

"The ape is this rough draft of man. Mankind have their gradations as well as the other productions of the globe. There are a prodigious number of continued links between the most perfect man and the ape."—JOHN WESLEY.

THE relation of man to his vertebrate kin is betrayed not only by his anatomy, his physiology, and his individual development, but by the facts of his geological history as well. True human fossils are comparatively rare, and correspondingly precious. Even prehistoric human remains, aside from examples of man's handiwork, are not common. The immediate ancestors of man very probably were not tree-dwellers; they lived chiefly on the ground though mostly in the forests. The fossil remains of all forest-living animals are rare because the conditions are not conducive to easy fossilization. Even when ancestral man came to occupy the open plains, he was alert to escape the sandstorms and floods by which the remains of many kinds of animals have been entombed. It was only after the time when the custom of burial arose that human remains began to be more commonly preserved, and these are chiefly portions of the skull, jaws and teeth, which on account of their massiveness and hardness are more resistant than other portions of the skeleton to the solvent action of the elements.

Evolution and Christian Faith

Man has had a long ancestral line of his own which paralleled that of the apes. He is not descended from any known form of ape either living or fossil, but both the human and the ape lines arose side by side from more lowly forms. So far, the exact forms involved in this early history are problematical, though *Propliopithecus,* from the Oligocene of northern Egypt, is at least structurally ancestral to the higher apes and man. Osborn thinks that from such a form at least four lines of descent originated leading respectively to man, to the living orang-utans of Borneo and Sumatra, to the gibbons of Asia and the Malay Archipelago, to the chimpanzees and to the gorillas of central Africa. Three of these lines found their safest homes in the trees, and are now very far removed from the larger-brained, walking line that adopted a life on the ground and finally developed into man. These semi-human ancestors of ours walked only partially erect for a very long time, perhaps as far as the Miocene period. Of course previous to them lived the pre-human tree-dwelling forerunners of the human race. An epitome of the geological history of the Primates, based on the account given by Schuchert, runs about as follows: In the American Eocene (Wasatch) are found the remains of the oldest lemurs, while diminutive but true monkeys are not found until in the Bridger formation. The close of the Eocene witnessed the extinction of all the Primates in North America. *Propliopithecus,* apparently the progenitor of all the later man-like apes,

THE GEOLOGICAL HISTORY OF MAN

appears in the later Oligocene of Egypt, whence it spread in the early Miocene into Europe. In western Europe it gave rise to *Pliopithecus,* which in turn produced the still larger *Dryopithecus.* In the upper Miocene this line divided into that which remained among the tree-tops and finally produced the gibbons, orangs, chimpanzees and gorillas; and secondly, into that which took more and more exclusively to living upon the ground and finally became human.

The latter line evidently spread, like the former, into Asia and Africa, where the truly human species had its cradle.

The most ancient remains of man at present known are the primitive flints found in the Upper Pliocene at Foxhall in East Anglia (England). These occur at two levels, 16 and 18 feet respectively below the surface. "They include hafted specimens, side-scrapers . . . , a number of arrowhead-like *pointes,* also borers and scrapers of the ordinary type." No remains of human bones have yet been found at this horizon, but the flints indicate a workmanship of no mean order. At the very least they indicate that tool-making man existed in England in the late Pliocene.

In Asia the most primitive of the human line, or the most human of the ape-line, is represented by the fossil remains of the ape-man, *Pithecanthropus erectus,* found by Dubois in 1891, in an early Pleistocene deposit at Trinil, Java. It was associated with a great number of mammalian bones of species now extinct. The Pithecanthropus remains comprise the upper part of the skull, three molar teeth, and the entire left femur. They indicate a long-headed creature with a low crown and prominent brow-ridges; while the volume of the brain-cavity (between 850 and 950 cc.) indicates a brain of about 28 ounces in weight, the forehead was more receding than in the modern chimpanzee. As the maximum brain capacity of the gorilla is only about 20 ounces (in volume between 500 and 600 cc.), and the average human brain weighs about 49 ounces (1450 to 1550 cc.) and the smallest normal brain of living man is probably never less than 30 ounces, it is clear that the brain capacity of the Pithecanthropus is more than half-way between the apes and man. It is estimated from the size and shape of the femur that the Pithecanthropus was about 5 feet 6 inches high, walked nearly erect, and may have had the rudiments of vocal speech. The receding forehead indicates that this creature had very limited frontal lobes, the seat in the brain of the higher intellectual powers, and had therefore small reasoning powers, although the special senses of touch, taste, and sight were seemingly more acute than in modern man. Pithecanthropus was probably governed very largely by instinct and thus lived more on the animal plane. His erect posture, however, indicates the liberation of the hands from any part in locomotion and, as will be indicated in the succeeding chapter, this was an immense gain, a factor largely responsible for the development of the intellect. His teeth were more human than ape-like, and indicate that his food was masticated in much the fashion of modern man, and very likely was not far different from that of savage races now living in the tropics.

The next oldest human remains were found in 1907 in some river deposits of sand seventy-nine feet below the surface at Mauer, near Heidelberg, not far from the Rhine, in Baden. The specimen comprises only the lower jaw with all its teeth, yet it displays a combination of characters not found in any other specimen living or fossil. There is no chin prominence and in shape the whole jaw is more nearly like that of some large ape, yet the teeth are distinctly human. They are rather smaller than might have been expected from the massiveness of the jaw, and though somewhat primitive in form, are clearly not simian. The whole jaw indicates a generalized type lower in the scale of development than the Neanderthal type, described below. Associated with it was an extensive series of warm-climate animals, such as the straight-tusked elephant, Etruscan rhinoceros, primitive horse, bison, wild cattle, bear, lion, etc., all species now extinct and serving to establish the age of the jaw as second interglacial, or approximately 350,000 years old. In the same deposits were found flint implements (eoliths) of the crudest workmanship, if indeed they had been consciously fashioned at all.

There were recently found by the miners of the Broken Hill Mining Company, in Rhodesia, South Africa, the skull and other portions of the skeleton of a primitive type of man that had lain under a huge pile comprising many tons of the bones of other animals, some sixty feet below the surface. This find was exhibited at the 1921 meeting of the Anatomical Society of Great Britain by Dr. A. Smith-Woodward, of the British Museum, in whose custody the specimen now is. Associated with the skull there were also found some very crude instruments of flint and quartz of human workmanship. According to a report of the Association meeting recently published in *Science* (February 3, 1922, page 129) "the skull is in some features the most primitive one that has ever been found; at the same time it has many points of resemblance to (or even identity with) that of modern man. Fortunately, the face is perfectly preserved, the supra-orbital region is astonishingly gorilla-like, in its enormous size and its unusually great extension laterally; the cranium is almost flat on top, extending backward from the huge supra-orbital ridges rising only a little above the level of their upper borders. It is very broad in the back, however, so that its total capacity is surprisingly large." This would seem to indicate a creature in whom the higher intellectual powers were relatively little developed, while the sensory and instinctive centers of the brain were probably much greater than in modern man. "Another striking thing to be seen at the back of the skull is the evidence (in the size of the ridges and the contrasting deep impressions), of the tremendous and powerful mass of neck muscles the creature must have had. This is one of the points upon which is based the opinion that the skull is the most primitive yet found." . . . "Dr. Smith-Woodward pointed out the fact that the suture of the nasal with the frontal bone is in a straight line rather than at a definite angle as in the apes; he also called attention to the small tubercle of bone in the mid-line of the nasal fossa which . . . is distinctly a human trait." The face was exceedingly long, for the distance from the floor of the eye-orbit to the margin of the upper jaw is phenomenally great, as was also the case with the upper lip, since the length from the floor of the nasal cavity to the base of the teeth at the edge of the upper jaw is likewise very great. In other words, the creature's face must have had much of the aspect of the modern gorilla with its strongly prognathous features. "The palate is beautifully arched, and the teeth form a perfect horseshoe at its border. The wisdom tooth is reduced in size—another point in common with modern man and never found before in a fossil skull." . . . There is "unmistakable evidence of dental caries, and even of abscesses at the roots of the teeth." . . . "In contrast to the Neanderthal man . . . , this man is believed to have maintained the upright position, because the femur is relatively straight and when fitted to the tibia (which was also found) presents a perfectly good, straight leg." . . . "Dr. Eliot Smith at least is quoted as leaning to the belief that further study will reveal the fact that "the missing link" in the ancestry of man is repre-

EVOLUTION AND CHRISTIAN FAITH

sented in this individual—referring, of course, to European man. The Neanderthal man would then represent a branch off of the main ancestral tree."

In 1912 remains of a very ancient man were found in the plateau gravels at Piltdown, near Fletching, in Sussex, England. The find consists of the greater part of a skull, which, however, was injured and partly lost. The fragments, consisting of portions of the cranial walls, nasal bones, and a canine tooth, came into the hands of Dr. A. Smith-Woodward, of the British Museum, who has pieced them together, and has thus been able to restore the greater part of the skull. The braincase is typically human, though with unusually thick walls, and has a capacity of nearly 43 ounces (1300 cc.). The skull is relatively short, and while the forehead is relatively high, it lacks the prominent brow-ridges so well-marked in Pithecanthropus and apparently also in the Rhodesian man. The Piltdown skull was associated with very ancient types of paleolithic tools, and with a warm-climate fauna including the hippopotamus and other animals now extinct in Europe. Geologists compute its age as somewhere about 125,000 years. The Piltdown man, while of a higher type than any which preceded him, "was still a primitive slayer, though keener than any of his animal associates, and was destined through the manufacture of better implements to become a hunter of a higher order." (Schuchert).

In 1856 the Neanderthal valley in Rhenish

THE GEOLOGICAL HISTORY OF MAN

Prussia was the scene of one of the most interesting discoveries of prehistoric human remains. Here in a little cave in the limestone walls of the valley was found a perfect skeleton of a man, since called *Homo primigenius* (or *neandertalensis*), but those who found it were so little skilled in the preservation of such a specimen that it was badly injured and partly lost. What remains has been carefully preserved in the museum at Bonn. Since then more than a dozen other specimens of the race, including adults of both sexes, as well as children, have been found in caverns in Belgium, France, Gibraltar, and Croatia. Huxley has given a classic description of this people in these words:

"The anatomical characters of the skeletons bear out conclusions which are not flattering to the appearance of the owners. They were short of stature but powerfully built, with strong, curiously curved thigh bones, the lower ends of which are so fashioned that they must have walked with a bend at the knees. Their long depressed skulls had very strong brow-ridges; their lower jaws, of brutal depth and solidity, sloped away from the teeth downwards and backwards, in consequence of the absence of that especially characteristic feature of the higher type of man, the chin prominence."

This long-lived race was in existence for many thousand years, and probably became extinct not to exceed twenty to twenty-five thousand years ago. In the cold glacial climate they were contemporary with the hairy elephant (mammoth), the bison, horse, and reindeer, all of which probably served them for food. According to Schuchert, they were a savage-looking race of stout build, short stature, averaging about 5 feet 3 or 4 inches, with disproportionately large heads. They were skilful enough to make fairly good stone implements and knew how to kindle a fire, for hearths occur in their cave abodes. The face was singularly unlike any existing race, with an unusually large and broad nose, a very wide upper lip, and a continuous brow-ridge running from temple to temple at the base of the forehead. This last character marks them off from all other types of man. Lull considers the Neanderthal skull as in many characteristics nearer the apes than to modern man. Though the brain is surely human in size, its proportions are less like those of modern man than those of the apes. "The chest is large, and robust, the shoulders broad, and the hand large, but the fingers are relatively short, the thumb lacking the range of movement seen in modern man." The powerful leg, with its short shin and clumsy foot, was clearly not adapted for rapid running. Moreover, a curvature of the leg was correlated with a lack of the neck curvature in the spine, characteristic of modern man. "One of the most remarkable features in connection with this race, however, was the very reverent way in which the dead were buried, with an abundance of (food), ornaments, and finely worked flints. This (ceremonial burial) can have but one interpretation,

THE GEOLOGICAL HISTORY OF MAN

the awakening within this ancient type of the instinctive belief in immortality."

After the close of the Glacial Period, somewhere from fifteen to twenty-five thousand years ago, there appeared in Europe "men of the human species (*Homo sapiens*) who were still hunters but who possessed far greater skill in the making of stone and bone implements, and who also engraved and painted pictures of many kinds of animals in the caves of France and Spain." These men, however, represent two diverse races; the first a tall people, averaging six feet in height in the males, with long arms and long legs. They had a well-fashioned foot and were evidently swift and enduring runners. The head was remarkably long, with a cranial capacity ranging between 52 and 56 ounces, in this respect surpassing the average European today. The face was wide and short, with extremely prominent cheek-bones; the orbits of the eyes were wider than long, and depressed; the brow-ridges were strong; the palate was broad; the incisor teeth in both jaws had a tendency to project forward while the chin was narrow and pointed. This race is generally referred to as the Crô-Magnon.

The second of these two races, the Grimaldi, specimens of which have been found in association with the Crô-Magnons, was negroid in character, shorter of stature, 5 feet 2 to 5 inches, with the lower limbs extremely long, the nose flat and broad, protruding jaws, and a somewhat retreating chin. Schuchert thinks that they were probably related to the living Bushmen of Africa, while Osborn notes the resemblances between the Crô-Magnons and the modern Sikhs of India and the Eskimos. In short, this clearly dominant race was Asiatic rather than African in the sum of its physical characters. The very interesting association of these two distinct types suggests the possibility that human slavery may have existed even in those prehistoric times, when the Crô-Magnons chased the wild horse and reindeer in France and Spain, where the climate was much colder than it is at present.

Schuchert notes that their "implements are of the newer Paleolithic type, that is the workmanship of the flints is better and constantly improves with time, and the race had many more kinds of tools to serve more purposes. They also used bone for awls and ivory for skewers and ornaments, and made spears, bows and arrows, and fur garments. Themselves they ornamented with marine snail shells and teeth of mammals, and later with beads, bracelets, and other objects manufactured out of shell and ivory."

"Armed with better weapons of the chase and a wider knowledge of their use, the Crô-Magnons were able to take better advantage of their environment. Under these circumstances, they had more ease and time for reflection, and we witness in them the birth of the fine arts. Sculpture and drawing appear almost simultaneously, and later comes painting. This art we find preserved in the caves of France and Spain, the art of one period

THE GEOLOGICAL HISTORY OF MAN

being overlaid by that of later times, and as time goes on the workmanship is greatly improved. Animals of many kinds are depicted, at first outlined in black, then engraved on the walls and even on the ceilings of the dark caves; later were added polychromes in red, brown, black, and several shades of yellow. The pigments were of mineral origin and were mixed with grease. These artists also engraved animals on stone, bone, and ivory. The human figure appears only in the later paintings, and in these, garmented women are seen herding cattle and men chasing wild animals." (From Schuchert, "Historical Geology," pp. 973-4.)

The Crô-Magnons, some of whose descendants seem to survive today in Dordogne, at Landes near the Garonne in Southern France, and at Lannion in Brittany, were evidently well advanced toward civilization, perhaps not far, if any, below the Gauls whom Caesar encountered. They were certainly partly, at least, contemporaneous with the Neanderthal race, which Osborn thinks may have owed its extinction in no small degree to contact with them. After the decline of the Crô-Magnons, other Asiatics crowded into Europe, the dark-skinned long-headed race now occupying the shores of the Mediterranean, and the round-headed Alpine type. This invasion in the Upper Paleolithic, perhaps ten thousand years ago, has had its influence on the development of European civilization to this very day. While the men still delighted in the chase, they were pastoral enough to hold herds of cattle and flocks of sheep and goats, by means of which they were assured against famine, and thus had opportunity for the development of agriculture, religion, government, and learning. With them came finally the civilizations of Greece and Rome, and the impressive march of events that eventuated into modern Europe.

CHAPTER VI

THE ROLE OF THE HAND IN
THE EVOLUTION OF MAN

"The free use of the arms and hands, partly the cause and partly the result of man's erect position, appears to have led in an indirect manner to other modifications of structure."

—DARWIN, *Descent of Man.*

IN this sentence Darwin cautiously expresses an idea which is important enough to receive greater emphasis than has been accorded it by most writers. It is a rather curious fact that while much attention has been given to the evolutionary history of the limbs in the horse and other hairy quadrupeds, relatively little has been paid the human hand. And yet it can be demonstrated that this organ has probably played a greater rôle than any other except its reciprocals, eyes and brain, which have mutual relations with it. MacFarlane is the only recent author who seems to have given this matter any consideration. In other fields the importance of the hand has been given recognition, as witness the most noticeable tendency in present-day educational circles, the recognition of the fundamental importance of the hand in relation to mental development. The whole underlying motive of "vocational education" is *the training of the brain through the hand*. One great value of science from a purely educational point of view lies in the laboratory work which engages the hand and through that the development of the most important of the mental powers.

Probably before the simian ancestors of man descended from the tree-tops to live upon the ground, in the old *Propliopithecus* days, the hand was occasionally diverted from its chief function as an organ for climbing and employed to break off fruit, which, still held in the hand, was used for food. Later still, perhaps at first as the result of accident, branches were broken off, and some of these lodging in the crotch of the tree became the crude foundation or platform on which to rest; in time, this was consciously done, as the orang and chimpanzee have been observed to do at the present time. From this habit it was but a step to that of using such broken off branches as weapons to be hurled at some enemy below. We may be sure that every such experience was registered in the brain tissue in the form of a better-developed association tract. The development of the frontal and parietal lobes of the brain, where the association centers concerned in movements of the hand and arm are located, is well marked in the higher man-like apes, although much inferior still to the corresponding parts in man. When the pro-human stock took to a terrestrial mode of life, in all probability this process had already gone on farther than in the present-day anthropoids. But the new conditions of life on the ground immediately brought about the necessity for increased use of the hands, and it is clear that this could only be attained through the adoption of the upright posture and the further liberation of the hands from any necessary part in locomotion.

The necessity of defense against beasts of prey must early have led to a more extensive employment of broken limbs of trees as weapons. At first any convenient limb picked up by chance from the ground was made use of; then doubtless experience soon taught the advantages of a heavier branch from which all side branches and twigs had been removed. Each such gain in experience reacted upon the brain by the establishment of new association paths in the frontal and parietal lobes. Early it was discovered, no doubt, that other objects than limbs of trees could be made into efficient weapons, so that loose stones were used when an unexpected attack of an enemy occurred in a situation where a club was not immediately available. Experience readily proved the superiority of a small rounded stone for throwing at a distance. Skill in throwing such weapons would soon have followed their use—skill acquired through the establishment of new association paths in the cortex of the frontal and parietal lobes of the brain. This involved also correlated development of the optic centers, for the eye would become more and more a necessary element, since to be effective a correct judgment of distance is needed in the hurling of a stone against an enemy or a beast desired for food. Every act of this sort, involving hand, eye and brain, brought about further action, reaction, and interaction of these parts, resulting not only in greater development of these organs individually, but also further correlation between their association centers, or in other words greater intellectual powers. The struggle for existence naturally put a premium on the increased capacity for making these new associations, and each generation therefore would consist more and more of those individuals in whom this capacity was the better developed.

The use of the club and stone in time resulted in the discovery that the two together, the stone tied to the end of the club, gave increased effectiveness as a weapon, and so was invented the familiar war-club. The accidental splitting of the stone when hurled in this way, leaving a relatively sharp edge, was found to be even more effective, since by its use there was added to the crushing force of the impact of the weight, the cutting and splitting power of the sharp edge. That this account is not altogether a product of the writer's imagination, the crude eoliths so often found in various spots in both the Old and New Worlds abundantly testify. This use of the sharp edged flint was a discovery that undoubtedy soon led to the establishment of a new association tract in the brain, and for some time Eolithic man made use of such accidentally formed ax-heads. Eventually, perhaps not for a millennium however, for new inventions came slowly, but inevitably, the idea arose of purposively splitting or flaking flint nodules, when suitable objects in nature were not readily available (perhaps even in those early Paleolithic times, "necessity was (already) the mother of invention!"), and the art of manufacturing the crude tools of Paleolithic time arose. At first no doubt, weapons were the instruments desired and made, but it was early discovered that a sharp edged flint was more effective than the bare hands and teeth in removing the skins from slain animals. From such a simple beginning the manufacture of tools for the arts of peace began. Every new discovery gave increased skill to the hand by the establishment of new association paths in the cortex of the frontal and parietal lobes of the brain, thus leading man farther along on the path that brought him up and away from his non-progressive simian cousins. Each such advance in brain development brought about an increase in alertness, greater mental power, that could not but have been an advantage in the struggle for existence to those possessing it, and the consequent elimination of those in whom the capacity for this development was not so marked.

Eolithic man undoubtedly was acquainted with fire started in a natural way by lightning or from volcanic sources. No doubt he often warmed himself on chilly days by the smoldering embers of a tree that had suffered the stroke of Jove's thunderbolt. Possibly he may have early learned to preserve fire obtained from such a source by feeding it with dried branches picked up in its neighborhood. After he became a cave-dweller it would have been the natural thing for him to carry a burning brand to that cave and by that means establish a fire which rendered life there more comfortable and endurable. But for a long time man apparently knew not how to kindle a fire for himself. At last some time while pounding flints together in the manufacture of flakes for weapons or tools, the flying sparks caught some dry grass or leaves and started a fire. Such an accidental occurrence had most momentous consequences. Thus through the work of his hands man acquired the means for the production of fire, a source of energy that at once put him far in advance of all the beasts of nature. He soon discovered in the attempt to extinguish a fire with water that flint nodules hot from roasting in the flames were easily and readily split by the application of cold water. This discovery increased the ease with which his weapons and tools could be made and greatly reduced the labor involved. Reflection upon these discoveries led to increased development of the association paths and this in turn reflexly to increased mentality.

Early man doubtless plucked the ripe heads of wild grasses and cereals and ground them, chaff and grain together, between his teeth like the beasts of the field. No doubt he soon noticed that his hands in gathering the heads removed more or less of the chaff and it was but a small, but momentous, step to the rubbing of the heads between the hands so as to thresh the grain and free it from the chaff. For a long time doubtless, this slow and laborious process served its purpose, but eventually reflection brought the idea of pounding and rubbing larger quantities of the grain in a vessel, at first a mere cavity or depression in a rock, and so threshing machines were invented. Inevitably some of the grain would be broken and crushed, and the discovery followed that such broken grain was more readily masticated than when unbroken. This led to the fashioning of grinding mills, worked by hand and crude at first, but eventually more and more refined as the inventive power of the mind developed. Possibly through the heat generated by this frictional method of threshing grain, the chaff was occasionally set on fire, and man had discovered a second method of obtaining this valuable asset. Every such discovery was the means for the establishment of additional association paths in the cortex of the frontal and parietal lobes and led man still farther on the road toward the goal of civilization.

Man was even in his pre-human stage more or less of a gregarious being, delighting in the association of his fellows. At this time he doubtless had a series of vocal sounds by which he expressed his emotions and various simple ideas. This is no more than can be seen today in many of the lower animals, but as man increased in mental power, and his manner of life became more complex, he more and more felt the desire to communicate his ideas to his fellows. The simplest means of this communication was through the work of his hands and he scratched crude pictures upon the limestone walls of his cavern home, upon shells, sticks, and other suitable objects. In so doing he doubtless noticed the peculiar sounds made by the instruments he was using, so how natural that he should eventually imitate these sounds, and thus arose a simple form of articulate speech. Imitation of the cries of the wild animals around him sufficed at first to indicate the same to his associates, and thus began the development of those centers in the cortex concerned with speech. From imitation of natural sounds, in time, man went to the invention of arbitrary sounds to indicate objects of inanimate nature and true language thus arose. But in all this the hand played a preeminent part, for in the early stages when words were few, gesture was brought into use and the hand was the direct means for conveyance of many ideas for which words were lacking. MacFarlane ("The Causes and Course of Organic Evolution," p. 588) has a pertinent paragraph that may be quoted at this place in support of the view here expressed. He says:

"According to eminent philologists the root words of the three great types of human language amount to from 120 to about 500. Thus Max Müller reduced all Sanskrit words to 121, and regarding these Romanes truly remarks, a "most interesting feature of a general kind which the list presents is that it is composed exclusively of verbs." This peculiarity also of the ultimate known roots of all languages, which shows them to have been "expressions of actions and states, as distinguished from objects and qualities," is important. But a most striking circumstance is that of the total number about 68 or 70, or more than 60 per cent are wholly connected with motion of the hand or arm. Thus to abstract the first twenty-five, of which such is true, we have "dig, weave (or sew) crush (or pound), sharpen, smear, scratch, divide (or share), cut, gather, stretch, mix, scatter, sprinkle, shoot (throw at), pierce, (or split), join (or fight), tear, smash, measure, kindle, milk, pour, separate, glean, and cook." From spoken to written language is but a short step, which however involves further use of the hand.

In short, we may easily see that in the development of those characteristics in which man differs most from other animals, viz., in the greater development of the frontal and parietal lobes of the brain, in the possession of articulate speech, as well as in the possession of greater mental power, this superiority has come about directly or indirectly from the use of his hand as such. The most momentous day in the history of human kind was that on which pro-man adopted the upright posture, and thus liberated his hands for uses other than locomotion. From the latter have followed all the advances which he has made in mind, body, and in the arts; indeed, all civilization has inevitably come from manual dexterity.

CHAPTER VII

SOME DISADVANTAGES OF THE UPRIGHT POSITION

THAT the upright position is not natural to man is clearly manifest by the difficulty which every child experiences in learning to maintain it. In no other species does the young have to learn by a long and laborious process of conscious effort to acquire the usual posture of the adult. In most cases the young very early become almost or quite as adept in locomotion as the parents. This is particularly well shown in those forms in the case of which safety depends on speed in the escape from enemies. A few hours at most enables the young colt to trot at its mother's side and to keep up the pace for long intervals of time.

That man has adopted the upright position despite the difficulty of learning to maintain it, is sufficient evidence that it has compensating advantages, and it is clear that it enables him to extend the horizon of his vision so as earlier to see the form and approach of a possible enemy, and furthermore, as already pointed out, it has freed his hands for other purposes than locomotion. Despite these obvious advantages, however, it cannot be gainsaid that there are corresponding disadvantages. Anatomically these are numerous and contribute their evidence toward the view of man's derivation from lower forms. This subject is one about which little has been written and what follows is intended to be a suggestive outline rather than an exhaustive treatment.

In the case of animals that go on all fours, the limbs are attached at the "four corners" of the body in such a way as to divide the load among them and thus to lighten the burden which each must assume. When man took to walking upon his hind legs, on the other hand, all the weight of body and head was thrown upon the posterior extremities. In order to support this weight relatively greater development was forced upon the hip bones and the legs, but this perhaps was not so serious as the various curvatures of the spine which also followed. Man is the only animal, with the partial exception of the anthropoid apes, in which the backbone is necessarily curved in order to render more easy the support of the weight of the trunk and head, and in those apes the amount of spinal curvature is in direct proportion to the uprightness of their posture.

But man has among the four curves in his backbone, one which even these apes do not have, and it is one which has more serious consequences than any of the others. This is that located in the small of the back just above the hip bones, and is directed toward the ventral (or front) side of the body, thus encroaching greatly upon the abdominal space, already over-crowded by the viscera

DISADVANTAGES OF THE UPRIGHT POSITION

which have sunk into it as the result of the upright position. Yet this particular spinal curvature could not be avoided if man were to walk upright. Aside from the so-called normal curvatures of the spine, it is clear that the pathological curvatures, so frequently the cause of distress and worse in man, are directly due to the inability of a relatively weak backbone to support the body in an upright position, and they are so extremely rare in the animals which go on "all fours" because in them the spinal column is not subjected to those strains which in man are the directly exciting causes of the trouble.

The thickening of the hip-bones that has undoubtedly resulted from the erect posture, together with the more solid unions among the six elements that make up the hip girdle, has had a still more serious effect upon man. This is the increased difficulty which the reduction in the size of the already narrow birth canal has placed in the way of the ready egress of the young during the process of parturition. In none of the lower animals is the labor and pain of birth even relatively so great as in woman. This is in part due to the relatively large size of the head of the unborn child, the direct result of the large brain whose development is indirectly, through the hand, the result of the upright position. The rotation of the human leg at the hip, from the normal position of the quadruped, accompanied by the retention of the large angle between the head and the shaft of the thigh bone, results not only in a mechanical inconvenience, but is also the reason why in old people a fracture at this place is not only of frequent occurrence but is often incurable.

Civilized man when he takes his ease in office or at home is prone to put his feet on the top of his desk or table, often to the annoyance of his wife. This tendency is due to the fact that the point of the hip bones which must support the body weight when he is seated with the trunk upright are too close together for comfort; in a quadruped they never serve such a purpose. Man therefore unconsciously seeks to support a portion of his weight on the small of his back and in this way relieves the uncomfortable pressure upon his hip bones. In woman the hip girdle is considerably broader than in man, hence the discomfort just mentioned is probably not so acute in her case, and so woman is not so prone to adopt the ungraceful sprawl so commonly assumed by her husband.

But it is in standing still that man most easily discovers the disadvantages of the unnatural posture he has assumed. Everyone has experienced the peculiarly fatiguing effects that follow from standing for any length of time in one place and in one position. In military organizations this fact is recognized and frequent changes of position are provided, but occasionally in ceremonies in which the men may remain at attention for long periods it has happened that some of the weaker have fainted from the strain. This fatigue is due to at least two faults in man's anatomical structure which clearly reveal that he was not originally in-

DISADVANTAGES OF THE UPRIGHT POSITION

tended to be a biped. The first of these is the manner of attachment of his over-heavy head to the upper end of his backbone. The skull is not so placed as to give an even balance, but on the contrary there is a constant tendency for the head to drop forward so that the chin may rest on the chest. In order to overcome this and to hold the head erect man constantly must make use of the muscles in the back of the neck and shoulders, and this shortly becomes very fatiguing without frequent change of position. The second anatomical fault that produces excessive fatigue when one remains long in a standing position is that which brings about the strain on the muscles of the abdomen, the lower back and thigh through the constant use of these muscles to prevent his falling over. In the quadruped with the four legs held under the body there is no such muscular strain, but in man with the legs stretched straight out behind parallel to the long axis of the body, the strain is excessive and consequently wearisome. Furthermore, the arch of the foot, while admirably adapted to quadrupedal locomotion, is very poorly fashioned for bipedal support. As a result the arches often "break down," and broken arches or flat-footedness is a very frequent condition, the ill effects of which are commonly recognized. There is little doubt that many affections of the joints, such as that long series generally grouped in the popular mind as "rheumatic," are more or less directly due to the results of the strains incident to the upright position.

Eye-strain is often largely due to the constant muscular effort necessary to secure coordination and convergence in vision. Likewise as a result of the upright position it is necessary for man to roll his eyes down toward the horizontal by action of the lower straight eye-muscles. That all these result in muscular fatigue is shown by the frequent necessity that everyone experiences of "resting the eyes" when engaged upon close work, by raising them and directing the sight for a time at distant objects. Moreover, it is well known that in sleep or after death the eye-balls tend to roll upward and to assume the normal position that is maintained by the quadruped. Even in death therefore man offers mute testimony to his lowlier origin.

In the quadruped the ventral body wall is strongest forward where the heaviest organs are located and where the muscular diaphragm and ribs assist in their support. But in assuming the upright position the weight of these organs is thrown on what is now the lowermost portion of the abdomen, where it is not only weakest in muscular development but where no aid is secured from the ribs or diaphragm. The result is the frequent dropping down of the viscera to the distress of their owner, the derangement resulting in stomach and intestinal disorders that interfere with digestion, cause the production of "gas in the stomach" and its attendant inconveniences, and to no little extent, results in chronic constipation and its accompanying evils. The heavy kidneys tend frequently to drop down and to become the so-called "floating kidneys" with the frequent consequences of twisted and deranged blood vessels and ureters, with serious effects upon the kidney itself and even more serious physiological effects upon the human being so affected. The atrophy or degeneration of these organs is responsible for serious functional derangements that may eventuate into disease and death.

Furthermore, the depression of the viscera into the abdominal cavity frequently leads to that painful form of rupture known as "inguinal hernia," a derangement unknown among quadrupeds. The pressure upon the great vein of the abdominal cavity following not only upon the greater column of blood which it must support in the upright position but also as a result of the increased pressure upon it of the additional load of the viscera, is very often directly responsible for disturbances in its dependent veins, resulting in hemorrhoids, varicocele, and varicose veins and ulcers of the leg. Many of the derangements of the reproductive organs "peculiar to women" are also due to the unnatural position of the organs of generation when the quadrupedal posture has been abandoned, as well as to the lack of ability on the part of the weak abdominal wall and the internal supports to hold them in place.

It is clear, then, from this hasty and incomplete survey that for the inestimable advantages man gained through the upright position in its influence upon the brain and its development, and its accompaniment, the greater mental power and attainments, he has paid and must continue to pay in pain, suffering, and the "sweat of his brow." Yet the advantages far out-weigh the disadvantages, and we would not, if we could, return permanently to our ancestral posture.

CHAPTER VIII

THE EMBRYOLOGY OF THE MIND

THE origin and development of the mind or soul in the individual is to many a matter of deep mystery, and explanations have been sought in various but usually entirely speculative directions. The explanations arrived at have varied all the way from the notion that mind is a material secretion of the brain to the idea that it is a miraculous product specially implanted by the Creator within the individual at some time, usually undetermined, either before or after birth. The psychologists have not gone to the root of the problem, for they have been content to begin with the child after birth and to trace his growth in mental power from that point on. The study of prenatal behavior has been more or less widely attended to with reference to the lower vertebrates, in which the higher manifestations of mentality do not exist, but no one had undertaken a study of the embryology of the mind in *mammals* until the present author began his investigations in that field some years ago. The scientific method must be adopted here also, and while the results obtained will be found to furnish *proximal* explanations, the *ultimate* cause of mind and life itself will be found only to recede to a greater distance, but not to be solved. This will be recurred to in a later chapter.

In order to set forth the author's point of view in a proper manner, it would be necessary to trace the principal developmental stages of the bodily structures in man or some other mammal. The limitations set by the purposes of this book, however, forbid anything but the briefest epitome of such an account. As has been said in a preceding chapter, every many-celled animal, *including man,* begins its development in the form of a *fertilized egg,* a single cell in which there are none of the structures characteristic of the adult, though in certain cases at least it may foreshadow the appearance of such structures by the presence of specific kinds of living matter, the so-called organ-forming substances, which give rise to specific tissues or organs of the adult. These organ-forming substances have a definite arrangement with reference to each other within the egg, a phenomenon indicated by what are technically called polarity and symmetry. The egg-cell furthermore is known in all cases to divide many times and so, as development proceeds, to produce the vast number of cell-units of which the adult organism is composed. Accompanying this process of cell-multiplication there goes on the differentiation of the cells to form the various kinds of tissues, such as nerve, muscle, bone, etc., and the correlated physiological division of labor as the result of which some tissues serve for protection, some for support, some for contraction, some for digestion, etc. That one kind of egg develops into a frog, another into a chick, and still another into a man, is due to the peculiar specific organization with which each begins, an organization that is inherited from the parents, and is ordinarily little modified by the environment. But after all is said, it is still true that the earliest differentiations of the various kinds of eggs are relatively few and simple in comparison with the manifold complexities of the adult.

Living matter (technically called *protoplasm*) in the simplest form known possesses certain fundamental characteristics among the most important of which are the properties of (1) *organization*, (2) *metabolism*, (or the power to change food materials into living substance, to liberate energy by the breaking down of previously formed substances, and the elimination of the waste products), (3) *reproduction*, and (4) *sensitivity*. Of these the last three are clearly related to the first as function to structure. That is to say, metabolism, reproduction, and sensitivity are properties of the organization inherent in protoplasm. Of these three inherent functions of the simplest living matter, the last, sensitivity only, concerns us here. Sensitivity may be defined as the property of protoplasm on account of which it is able to receive the effects of changes in its environment (in the broadest sense of that term), to store up these effects for a longer or shorter time, and to react or respond to them by some kind of change within the protoplasm itself. It is a phenomenon familiar to every student of elementary biology. For example, the *amoeba,* one of the simplest of one-celled animals, reacts in a very simple way toward most stimuli, usually by moving toward or away from the source of stimulation. But even this very simple case reveals a certain degree of complexity. The simplest possible condition would be one where the protoplasm always reacts in the same way to every stimulus, no matter what its nature. It is easy to see why no such simple case is ever observed. Any bit of living matter that would react toward poison or other deleterious condition in the same way as toward food or any other beneficial stimulus, would soon be eliminated. Consequently the very lowliest organisms, such as bacteria and the unicellular animals, exhibit what is termed *differential sensitivity.* In other words, they discriminate in a crude way between stimuli of different kinds, or between different degrees of stimulation of the same kind. Thus light has a stimulating effect upon most organisms, some of which respond by moving towards it when it is weak, or away from it when it is strong; or they move toward light from one end of the spectrum and away from that at the other end. The unicellular organisms (or in fact organisms of all kinds) find a certain temperature most agreeable. If inclosed in such a way that they can move between points hotter and colder than that most agreeable, they will be found to leave the extremes and to congregate at or near the point where the temperature suits them best. Similar reactions are observed when the organisms are stimulated by weak and strong acids, the positive and negative poles of a battery, violet and red rays of light, etc. While within limits most organisms tend to respond in the same way to the same stimulus, this is not universally true; some will respond to a stimulus to which others may be apparently wholly indifferent.

Experiments upon the reproductive cells of the higher animals show that they exhibit this same fundamental property of *differential sensitivity*. Sperm-cells, (the male reproductive cells), for example, have been found to move toward a weak solution of formic acid, toward weak alkalis and alcohol, and toward extracts of the eggs of their own species, while toward extracts of the eggs of other species they are either indifferent or react negatively by moving away from the stimulating substance. The eggs of most of the higher animals are not capable of locomotion, possibly due to the large load of inert food material which they contain, but in the case of hydra and other simple forms the egg resembles an amœba, moving about and displaying the fundamental properties of protoplasm found in that lowly organism. But within the egg-cells of even the vertebrates movements of their substance occur, and by these movements the sensitivity of the egg can be determined. Thus, if one prick the surface of a freshly laid frog's egg with a fine pointed needle, it will be found that the material at the surface of the egg flows toward the point of stimulation, accumulating there until it forms a little mound which in size would be comparable to Mt. Everest were the egg magnified to the volume of the earth. In other words, the amount of this movement of egg-material is relatively enormous.

A similar response is made to the attack of the first male reproductive cell (sperm-cell) that reaches the surface of the egg. That the egg really possesses *differential sensitivity* is shown by the fact that no such reaction follows the attachment of the second or later male-cell. After the fertilization of an egg by a male-cell of the species, it and the cells which result from its division display similar phenomena. In response to stimuli originating either outside or inside the egg, the organ-forming materials are separated and distributed to other definite positions in the egg or in the cells derived from it. As one result of this differentiation it soon comes to pass that certain portions of the young embryo are sensitive to some sorts of stimuli to which other parts may not respond at all, and *vice versa,* the final result being the formation of organs of special sense by which only stimuli of a particular sort are received. In short, beginning with *general sensitivity* in the *germ-cells,* or at most *differential sensitivity,* there are developed from these, *pari passu* with the development of the organs of the embryo, the *special senses. The foundation of all mental activity lies in sensations,* such as those of sight, hearing, touch, taste, smell, equilibrium, temperature, etc.

THE EMBRYOLOGY OF THE MIND

The simplest of all responses to a stimulus is *movement*, either toward or away from the source of stimulation. In the simplest plants or animals, and frequently also in higher forms where movement is possible, such automatic reactions are termed *tropisms*. The reactions of the reproductive cells already mentioned are tropisms, as well as the movements of cell-masses in embryonic development, such as, for example, the bulging in or out of the wall of a hollow sphere (*gastrulation*), the formation of folds or tubes in the establishment of the central nervous system or of the digestive tract. Indeed, the growth of certain structural elements, as for example that of the nerves, by which the *sensory* trunks find their way to their appropriate sense organs, while the *motor* portions of the same nerves go unerringly to muscles or glands, is clearly a case of *chemotropism* or a response to a chemical stimulus, as was shown some years ago by the observations and experiments of Professor Harrison of Yale University.

A tropism is a reflex reduced to its lowest terms. The transition from a simple tropism to a *reflex action* accompanies or results from the increase in structural complexity brought about by the formation of the tissues and organs of the embryo. Thus in the chick the heart is formed and begins to beat before there is any noteworthy development of muscle tissue in its walls, before there is any connection between it and the nervous system, and before there is any blood to be pumped by its contractions. The amnion, or sac filled with water, in which the embryo of reptiles, birds and mammals is suspended for the duration of the fetal period, likewise early begins rhythmic contractions which result in a rocking of the embryo to and fro as in a cradle, while there is no nervous connection involved. It is possible that a *habit* is thus early formed that accounts for the soothing effect that rocking in its mother's arms or in a cradle has upon the fretful baby. After the development of the nerves and nerve centers many other organs and parts of the growing embryo display even more complex movements, such as the opening and closing of the mouth accompanied by swallowing movements in the human fetus beginning during the fourth month of prenatal life. These are simply extensions of the tropism, but because of their increased complexity are termed *reflexes* or *reflex actions*.

When reflexes become so complex as to involve more than single organs or parts; especially when they have come under the direction of the nervous system and *concern the welfare of the organism as a whole rather than of a particular part,* they are termed *instincts* or *instinctive reactions*. For example, in the author's own investigations upon the developing mammal, it was found that the young before birth have the instinct for orienting themselves, or assuming a position when at rest such as bring the dorsal side of the body up; they also exhibit the swallowing reflex and have the sucking instinct sometime before birth. This probably accounts for the fact that the human fetus swal-

THE EMBRYOLOGY OF THE MIND

lows portions of the amniotic fluid and the various solids suspended in it during at least the last five months of prenatal life. Some other instincts no more complicated than these, so far as known, do not appear until after birth, though that the infant is capable of displaying them earlier is clear from the fact that seven-months babies nurse and develop other instinctive activities very nearly or quite as soon after birth as do those born at full term. *Differential sensitivity, tropisms, reflexes, and instincts form a succession of developmental stages in the individual, therefore, that is paralleled by the same phenomena as displayed by organisms at various levels of the animal scale. Furthermore, they appear in the same order and are composed of the same sorts and grades of phenomena in individual development as they must have in the evolution of the species.*

The reaction of protoplasm to a stimulus frequently, if not always, is of two sorts. There is the immediate response or tropism already mentioned, and a more subtle, invisible response that manifests itself only after one or more additional stimuli have been encountered. This is what psychologists term the *"summation of stimuli,"* and the response to such a series is frequently different in kind or at least in degree from the reaction to a single stimulus. In other words, the *effect* of the first stimulus *persists* for a longer or shorter time in the protoplasm and may modify subsequent reactions. One may readily suppose that the response to a stimulus involves the formation of a new chemical compound in the protoplasm and that this substance is somewhat stable, being broken down again only gradually unless a second stimulus intervenes, but when the substance decomposes or is otherwise modified, there results a new sort of response on the part of the protoplasm. Or, one may conceive of the effect of the first stimulus as being purely physical in nature, analogous to the change or "set" that takes place in metals when subjected to long mechanical strain. At any rate, whatever be the real nature of this phenomenon, *protoplasm has the property of recording in its structure the effects of a stimulus and by this modifying a future reaction to a second stimulus of the same or different sort. Nervous matter differs from ordinary protoplasm in that it has this property more highly developed; its reactions are the same in kind, but much greater in degree than are those of ordinary protoplasm.* That such a phenomenon is not limited to animals, is seen in a case well known to botanists, but which always arouses much interest in the mind of the observer. There is a notorious plant, called the "Venus Flytrap," which is carnivorous in habit, feeding upon flies and other insects that it catches for food. Its leaves have their tips modified into two flaps hinged at the midrib, and provided with a marginal row of spines and with a half-dozen or so sensitive hairs on the upper surface. When one of these hairs is touched no response is provoked, but a second stroke upon the same or a neighboring hair of the same leaf results

THE EMBRYOLOGY OF THE MIND

in the instant closing of the leafy flaps like the jaws of a steel trap. In 1892, MacFarlane, of the University of Pennsylvania, recorded the interesting observation that if the second stimulus followed the first *within three minutes* the trap was sprung instantly, but that if more than three minutes intervened, no response followed the second stimulus. In short, the effect of the first stimulus persists for only three minutes or less. Now, this phenomenon of summation of stimuli is clearly a primitive sort of *memory,* and one is justified in saying that this plant has a "memory" three minutes long. In other words, generalized protoplasm has not only sensitivity but also memory, and it would appear that specialized protoplasm also has this same property. In a general way this is shown by the fact that a muscle repeatedly exercised in the performance of a certain kind of work, not only grows in size, possibly a more or less direct response, but it also becomes more skilful, that is, it contracts more rapidly and accurately in response to the stimulus. That this power of registering past experiences is more highly developed in nerve cells than in other kinds is an example of the differentiation that always accompanies the physiological division of labor. The training of voluntary muscles that comes from long practice in walking, piano-playing, shooting of fire arms, archery, ball-pitching, talking, etc., is to be accounted for on the basis of this "organic memory," as Hering calls it, located in the muscles and nerve cells.

But one need not look only to the adult animal to observe this phenomenon. *The developing embryo displays it at all stages and in all its parts.* Indeed, development itself has been explained as a process of organic memory, and heredity, on this view, is simply the recollection by the embryo of processes undergone at the corresponding stage in the development of its ancestors. This idea may at first glance seem absurd or far-fetched, but the more closely it is examined the more fundamental does the conception appear to be.

This fundamental power of all protoplasm, the ability to store up for a time the effects of former stimuli, present to a greater degree in the highly differentiated matter of the nerve-cells, leads to that development of memory in the latter as the result of which associations are formed between the effects of different or successive stimuli; in short, it results in the production of that phenomenon which is termed *"associative memory."* Associative memory is certainly present in all the higher vertebrates, and is probably to be found in lower vertebrates and the higher invertebrates as well. The reproductive cells of the higher animals are endowed with protoplasmic and organic memory, and if they do not exhibit associative memory, at least the embryos or larvæ of some forms sooner or later in their development do possess the power of forming associations. At any rate all must agree that the human infant very early displays this power.

The step from associative memory to *conscious*

THE EMBRYOLOGY OF THE MIND

memory is a short one; whether it has been taken by the lower animals it is hard to decide, but that higher animals and infants possess it cannot be denied. Professor Jennings, of Johns Hopkins University, has devoted a great deal of time and study to the behavior of the lower organisms. He has found, for example, that when the unicellular *Paramecium* in swimming about in a dish of water comes into contact with an obstruction or with some irritating substance, its behavior is such that one may term it a *process of trial and error*. In other words, Jennings finds that under the circumstances cited, Paramecium backs away a short distance, rolls over on its dorsal side, and starts off in a new direction. There is here involved a long series of reflexes, such as the stopping of the motion of its minute hair-like organs of locomotion, and then the reversal of the direction of their beating, followed by a second pause and then the resumption of the stroke in such a manner as to drive the animal forward again. If this effort fails to eliminate the obstruction or irritation from the path of the creature, the process is repeated again and again until finally a path is found along which it is able to move without let or hindrance. To the observer, this behavior of Paramecium may appear purposive or intelligent, but further investigation shows that the reaction is, for the most part, at least, a fixed one, determined by the organization of the animal. Jennings and others have carried out this line of study with worms, starfishes, crayfish, lobsters, crabs and their relatives, insects and molluscs, as well as with various vertebrates such as fishes, frogs, turtles, birds and mammals. *In all these forms it has been found that the response of the animal to a new condition is not at first really purposive or intelligent, but rather a method of trial and error.*

With repeated trials, however, the animal gradually "learns," as it is commonly said, to eliminate the useless responses, and makes only those efforts that are successful. In other words, through the memory of the useful responses and the elimination of the useless ones the response of the organism becomes apparently purposive or, as is said, *intelligent. Intelligence, then, is a combination of differential sensitivity, reflex or instinctive reaction, and associative memory with the process of trial and error.* A single example of an experiment of the sort indicated may be cited, and that with an animal usually considered slow and stupid. Yerkes, when at Harvard, studied many such cases, but the *turtle* suits the purpose very well. As is well known this animal "is extremely sluggish in its movements. The impulse or incentive used to get the animal to work was that of escape. Instinctively the animal attempts to hide in some dark secluded place and will try to escape from confinement and go towards such a place. This combination serves very well for a motive. . . . The maze used consisted of a simple box 3 feet long, 2 feet wide, and 10 inches deep. It was divided into 4 portions by partitions 10 inches deep. At different points in the partitions holes 4 inches

The Embryology of the Mind

long and 2 inches deep were cut. This permitted the passage of the animal. After passing through the last partition the animal could get to its darkened nest of wet grass. A small speckled turtle learned this maze as follows: After wandering about constantly for 35 minutes, it *chanced* to find the nest, into which it immediately crawled and remained there until taken out 2 hours later. Experiments were made every two hours. On the second trial the nest was reached in 15 minutes. There was much less wandering. The time for the third trial was 5 minutes; for the fourth, 3 minutes and 30 seconds; during the first three trials the course taken was so tortuous that records of it were hard to obtain. There was an aimless wandering from point to point within each space, and from space to space. After the third trial the route became more direct. The tenth trial was made in 3 minutes and 5 seconds, with only two mistakes in turning. The time of the twentieth trial was 45 seconds; that of the thirtieth 40 seconds. In this case the course was direct, as was also true in the case of the fiftieth trip, which was made in 35 seconds." (Quoted from Watson's "Animal Behavior," p. 195.)

Any one seeing the turtle perform only for the fiftieth time would have said that it displayed considerable intelligence or at least that its movements in getting to the nest of wet grass were all purposive. Indeed, they were such, but that condition had been arrived at only as the result of trial and error, with the elimination of the useless movements and the recollection of the ones useful to attain the end sought. Porter's work with the English sparrow and other birds, Cole's study of the raccoon, Thorndike's investigation of the behavior of cats, dogs, and monkeys, to cite only a few well known examples, all show the same thing. Every observant parent knows that this is also true of infants. A baby lying in its crib reaches for the moon whose shining face it sees through the open window, or for a brightly colored object on the opposite wall of the room, until by repeated trials and failures, and a few trials and successes, it learns to appreciate distance and the length of its arms. It pops into its mouth all sorts of things pleasant or unpleasant, until it learns to know those which produce agreeable sensations and those which are disagreeable. The very act of putting things into its mouth is at first imperfect; the objects hit the cheek or chin or nose, rather than the mouth, and it is only by repeated efforts that the baby learns how to use its body properly. This is the same process of trial and error found in the dog, turtle, earthworm, or paramecium.

An animal in the course of time has many different experiences which are recorded in its memory; gradually similar experiences are associated, probably through the formation of brain paths, so that they tend to produce similar motor reactions. Many students of animal psychology think that the animal is strictly circumscribed by his experiences, that he cannot anticipate to any extent what may happen if the circumstances are not

THE EMBRYOLOGY OF THE MIND

very much like those already familiar. In other words, the animal is not capable of forming a *concept,* a generalized symbol of one experience, and of using it to forecast another event. In him associative memory and intelligence eventuate into a *recept.* Thus, Baldwin says that "a dog has a recept of the whip; so far as whips are not too different from one another, the dog will act in the same way toward all of them." This is therefore *reason* of a certain sort, but not the *abstract reason* of which man is capable. It is an intelligent use of associative memory and the results of trial and error in experience. It is certainly the type of reason exhibited by the child in its earlier years.

But the child very early learns, in imitation of his elders, to form symbols that stand for generalizations of his experiences, which usually take the form of words. To quote again from Baldwin: "He does not have, like the brute, to wait for successive experiences of like objects to impress themselves upon them; but he goes out toward the new, expecting it to be like the old, and so acting as to anticipate it. He thus falls naturally into general ways of acting which it is the function of experience to refine and distinguish. He seems to have more of the higher sort of what is called *apperception,* as opposed to the more concrete and accidental association of ideas. He gets concepts, as opposed to the recepts of the animals. With this goes the development of speech, which some psychologists consider the source of all man's superiority over the animals. Words become symbols of a highly abstract sort for certain classes of experiences; and moreover, through speech a means of social communication is afforded by which the development of the individual is enormously advanced."

These facts show plainly that *abstract reasoning* is a gradual acquirement; the higher animals and the very young child rise through associative memory and intelligence to what may be termed *receptive reason*. But here they part company, the child emerging into *conceptive* or *abstract reasoning,* to which probably no other animal has attained because it has not developed speech. Conklin puts the situation in these words, "in his development the human individual passes through the more primitive stages of intelligence, represented by the lower animals . . . ; the germ-cells and embryo represent only the stage of reflex behavior, to these trial and error and associative memory are added in the infant and young child, and to these the application of past experiences to new conditions, or reason, is added in later years."

There is no effect without a cause; an organism whether a paramecium or a man never displays an activity of any sort without there being some stimulus to call it forth. These stimuli may arise either outside or inside the organism. Paramecium and the earthworm, for example, like the germ-cells and embryos of higher forms are limited in the manner of their responses by the relative simplicity or homogeneity of their organization. With increased complexity of organization there comes

THE EMBRYOLOGY OF THE MIND

increased possibility of variation in the response to a stimulus. In the simpler organisms, most, though not all of the stimuli, are extrinsic—energy changes in the surrounding medium, and the responses are mostly direct. In more complex forms with associative memory, an extrinsic stimulus may be but the first in a long cumulative series, and the response may be far from direct. With the summation of stimuli there is introduced the possibility of modifying by later stimuli the effects of a previous one. This may occur in any one or more of several ways. Thus Whitman noted that a leech which normally hides away in dark situations under stones or chunks, will leave the shade even for bright sunlight, if it be hungry and the source of its favorite food, a turtle, be present. The stimulus of hunger modifies or nullifies the effect of the sunlight and completely changes the creature's behavior. Hunger is one of the very strongest stimuli, and yet in the case of the mud-puppy Whitman found that fear would so completely nullify the stimulus of hunger that the animal would starve to death even in the midst of plenty of the most tempting food rather than risk the sight of man. In short, conflicting stimuli, internal or external, may modify behavior. The formation of a habit, either voluntarily or under compulsion, as in the training of a dog or the education of a child, may limit the behavior to a single sort of reaction under circumstances where the particular stimulus under other conditions might result in any one of several responses. For example, the starfish ordinarily uses any one of its five arms in righting itself when it has been turned over on its back; but Jennings found that one which had been compelled habitually to use one certain arm for this purpose, afterwards continued to use that arm, though otherwise free to employ the other four. Natural selection undoubtedly has operated frequently in nature to compel the performance of an act in a certain way and thus to form a habit, until now the behavior of the animal is stereotyped. Such cases are the "lying low" or "playing 'possum" when pursued or attacked, displayed by familiar species of both vertebrates and invertebrates. On the other hand, associative memory and intelligence may result in the modification of behavior so that instead of making a response of immediate though minor importance, the organism may react in a way that is of little or no immediate advantage but of great future importance. Thus where there is possible a variety of responses, intelligent choice or *will* determines which reaction will be called forth by one or a series of stimuli. Thus *with will comes freedom of action,* not that one ever acts without a stimulus, an impossible hypothesis, but that through intelligence and reason intrinsic stimuli are introduced which may be more potent than the original external stimulus of the series. Thus, individually as well as racially, we have passed from the fixed or automatic reaction of the germ-cells or protozoan by gradual steps to *"freedom of the will," that is to intelligent, reasonable action.*

The Embryology of the Mind

And finally, the climax of the whole process is *consciousness,* the *awareness of our being.* This, too, is developed gradually in the individual; from a state of *unconsciousness* in the *embryo* there is a *transition* in *infancy* and *childhood* into *consciousness.* It is not necessary here to consider the nature of consciousness, whether it be merely the sum total of all the previously mentioned processes, or whether, like the relation of water to hydrogen and oxygen, it be a new product or synthesis of the others which have preceded it. Obviously there is also no need to argue with that school of psychologists who maintain that there is no such thing as consciousness! The point is simply this, that, granted the existence of what is commonly termed consciousness, or, in common terminology, the soul, it, too, has a period of development and only gradually attains maturity; it has been suddenly thrust upon or into neither the individual nor the race. It may be interesting to note that the supposed seat of consciousness is in the nerve cells of the cortex of the cerebral hemispheres, and that these cells never undergo a division after the birth of the child, but persist throughout his entire life. Can this fact furnish an explanation of the *continuity of consciousness,* or, in other words, our sense of *our own continuous personality?*

In conclusion, we would reaffirm the parallelism in development between mind and body; whatever one may conceive the ultimate relationship between the two to be, this much is sure: *they both develop concomitantly out of the egg. Both are the products of natural processes and there is no more reason for supposing a miraculous origin in the one case than in the other.* This conclusion, of course, is fraught with momentous practical and philosophical significance, and yet it has rarely been given the consideration it deserves. As Conklin has put it:

"We know that the greatest men of the race were once babies, embryos, germ-cells, and that the greatest minds in human history were once the minds of babies, embryos, and germ-cells, and yet this stupendous fact has had little influence on our beliefs as to the nature of man and of mind. We rarely think of Plato and Aristotle, of Shakespeare and Newton, of Pasteur and Darwin, except in their full epiphany, and yet we know that when each of these was a child he 'thought as a child and spake as a child,' and when he was a germ-cell he behaved as a germ-cell."

To argue that *both* the *body* and the *mind develop* from the *germ-cell* is quite a different thing from arguing that *matter and mind are identical. The germ-cell is just as truly living matter, indeed, the fertilized egg is just as truly a living being as is the adult man who develops out of it.* To associate the beginnings of mind with the germ-cell, to correlate its gradual development with that of the body, is to go no farther than we do in associating the mind with the body of the adult, a postulate universally accepted. *Mind is a function of living matter.* This in turn is not an affirmation that bodily structure causes the mind;

nor on the other hand that the mind causes the body. *Both are fundamental properties of living matter inherent in its organization.*

PART TWO
PHILOSOPHY

CHAPTER IX

THE PROBLEM OF ULTIMATE CAUSATION

IT is not an uncommon thing for students of biology to hear it stated that the doctrines of that science are "materialistic" in their implications. No one can deny that many biologists are or have been materialists in their philosophical views, but that a larger proportion of them are so inclined than are the devotees of other sciences, or of other professions in life, it would be difficult, if not impossible to prove. The trouble lies in that widespread confusion of mind as the result of which no distinction is made between *scientific mechanism* and *philosophic materialism*. The limitations of the scientific method are such that it can deal only with the data determinable through the senses; only those things which are *ponderable* or *measurable* fall within its purview. It must, therefore, seek all explanations in terms of matter and energy. Its explanations therefore are all *proximate;* it does not, it cannot, deal with *ultimate* causes. It is the philosopher, therefore, and *not* the scientist, or at least the scientist only when he goes beyond the confines of his field into philosophy, who can deal with the question of ultimate causation.

[125]

Evolution and Christian Faith

It is undoubtedly true that many have been misled by the arguments of philosophizing scientists, like Haeckel, into the belief that because biologists find a *human mechanism,* therefore all of man's personality is explicable in the terms of physics and chemistry. It is true that individual human behavior has a basis directly or indirectly in energy set free by the chemical processes involved in the oxidation of food or of the living substance itself in the cells of the brain and muscles. It is true as stated more or less distinctly in every biological textbook that man is an organism and like other organisms is made up of a large series of mutually dependent parts; that these parts or organs are associated in a complex manner for the performance of their various functions, and yet that they are all unified in such a way as to constitute a persistent integrated whole. It is also a fact that the organism differs from nonliving things in the matter of its chemical composition, not that it contains within itself any element not occurring elsewhere in nature, but that these elements are arranged in molecules of a complexity unknown in the inorganic world. The living individual is still further characterized by the manner in which it increases in size and bulk, taking materials unlike itself, breaking them up into simple chemical compounds out of which it manufactures the very complex molecules of living matter that are added to those already present within it, not by accretion on the outside as in the case of inorganic crystals, but by distributing these new molecules among the older ones already composing its structure. This is termed growth by *intussusception* and is one of the two or three absolutely distinguishing characteristics of protoplasm. Moreover, the behavior of the organism as a whole and of its individual parts as well is integrated, at least in the higher animals and man, by means of a unique mechanism, partly composed of the so-called *endocrine* glands with their peculiar chemical products, the hormones and chalones, and partly of that complex arrangement of cells and fibers known as the nervous system. And finally, the organic individual is governed by such physical laws as that of gravitation in just the same way as the non-living stone; it is an internal combustion engine which derives its energy directly from the fuel supplied it and indirectly from the sun's rays.

A consideration of such facts as these has often misled those without a clear insight, into the *philosophic* belief that every living thing, including man both as to his body and his mind, may be explained in terms of purely physical or chemical laws. The ideas of the conservation of matter and energy have been invoked to support the view that in man the only forces involved are the ordinary ones of the physicist and the chemist, which there act, react, and interact upon one another and upon the environment, modifying one another in various ways, assisting or hindering as the case may be, or even being changed from one form to another, without loss or addition. The idea is insisted upon frequently that accurate accounting for all the potential energy stored up within the organism or in the food which it assimilates, and for all the kinetic energy which it expends in the functioning of its muscular, glandular, nervous, and other organ-systems, would reveal an exact balance between the two sides of the ledger. In short, many students of biological phenomena are led into pure *philosophical materialism,* because on the surface of things, the organic mechanism *seems* self-sufficient. It appears to be complete in itself, to run entirely by means only of physical forces, and to leave no room nor necessity for a "soul." Individuality seems to be a phenomenon dependent upon conditions determinable, like ordinary physical or chemical phenomena, by resident forces; it does not seem to "require the presence or action of a non-perceptual agent." But *note carefully* that such a conclusion is a *philosophic,* not a *scientific* one. It is our purpose now to inquire whether the data of biology render such a conclusion in philosophy inevitable.

In the preceding chapter it was stated that man, at least, is possessed of self-consciousness. This consciousness is not a simple thing but may be analyzed into a series of phenomena that may be termed "states" or "moments" of consciousness, perceived directly or indirectly by means of the senses of touch, sight, hearing, etc. These units of consciousness follow one another like the waves of the sea and by them the individual is made aware of all those events which together constitute

THE PROBLEM OF ULTIMATE CAUSATION

his life experiences. We are each aware of these things in ourselves which we may describe to others, but the true explanation of them and of consciousness itself is perhaps not possible to finite minds. We cannot be sure, in a philosophic sense, of the existence and nature of consciousness in other minds than our own, except as they are manifested through the activity of those minds in the form of language, gesture, or other bodily function. This gives a validity to the common philosophic statement that the inner life of each individual is non-perceptual; to the fact of its non-perceptuality to others is due the seeming unreality of the soul of man.

It cannot be stated too emphatically nor too often that all the data of science are those of *conscious experience*. These data may be divided into two chief classes:

1. *Spatial phenomena,* those experiences which concern physical phenomena, the properties of matter and energy.

2. *Non-spatial phenomena,* those experiences which concern such apparently immaterial phenomena as thought and emotion.

But while consciousness may be analyzed into a series of successive "states" or "moments," its most characteristic property is not the separateness of these phenomena, but rather their *integration into a continuous and consistent whole.* Our conscious existence flows on like a river down which we float as in a drifting boat, and is not like the ties of a railroad track along which one walks with irregular steps. There is something that binds together, relates and controls the states of consciousness in each individual, something that acts as a committee of the whole. This something is the *ego,* the *will,* or the *soul* of man, as one may choose to name it. It is moreover something which is not bound by chronological necessity but which often removes past experiences from their exact time relationships, leaping from point to point in time often most erratically, or so it seems to one who does not carefully investigate the underlying psychological principles. This power of the ego to *dislocate the time order* of past experiences is the most convincing evidence of the *power* of the will; it proves that *freedom of the will* which is one of man's most priceless possessions.

Although we are accustomed to *think* of mind and body as separate entities, correlated or associated to be sure, yet clearly distinguishable in *thought,* it is impossible to find *scientific evidence* that they are separable in *reality.* Mental states are affected by physical conditions, just as bodily functions are affected. The health of the liver colors a man's thoughts just as surely as it may jaundice his skin; an overfull stomach retards mental activity just as surely as a burden on his shoulders slows down a man's steps. A blow on the head may temporarily or permanently put an end to all determinable mental phenomena just as certainly as it may cause the appearance of a bump on the scalp or a fracture of the skull. From the other side, certain emotional states may be

THE PROBLEM OF ULTIMATE CAUSATION

manifest in an increased rate of the heart beat and the consequent flushing of the face, or in the decrease in the glandular secretions. Protracted nervous strain may effect the retardation of the digestive function and the elimination from the body of the undigested food, just as, conversely, the latter condition, when brought about by purely physical means may hinder the flow of thought. In short, in so far as *science* can determine, mental states are subject to the same laws of cause and effect as are the purely bodily functions. This apparent relation of the body and the ego may be expressed by a mechanistic formula, in which we may let B stand for body and (e) for the ego, and the formula is this: $B(e)$. The body on this view, *i.e.*, the physical part of the human personality is the fundamental thing and conditions the ego, or produces it. But it requires no great amount of analysis for a biologist, not blinded by the tenets of materialistic philosophy, to perceive that this formula is inadequate to express all the relations between mind and body as found not alone in man, but in nature generally.

The behavior of an organism, at least in the case of man, depends to a large degree upon the operation of another factor that has not so far lent itself to recognition or analysis by the methods of the chemist or physicist. It has none of the properties of matter, it cannot be measured nor weighed, it occupies no dimensions in space; like the geometrician's point, it has neither length, breadth, nor thickness. By no apparatus of the physicist's devising can it be directly transformed into heat, light, electricity, nor any other form of physical energy. And yet it may and usually does so modify an organism's behavior that the observer is unable to foretell from a minute and exhaustive knowledge of the physical make-up and processes of that organism what it will do under any given set of physical conditions. The ego is so related to the body and its activities as to give a result that may be wholly different from that which would be produced under the same antecedent conditions without consciousness. Hit a ball with a club, and the physicist, from data concerned with the weight, size, form, etc., of club and ball, with the angle at which the two come into contact, etc., can predict exactly the course of the ball through the air, the distance it will travel, and the exact point at which it will strike the ground. Knowing the elasticity of the ball and the resistance of the ground he can determine the number and extent of the bounds the ball will make before coming to a final state of rest.

But let the same club be used on a dog or man, and the results cannot be so calculated. The dog may tuck his tail between his legs and run howling away, or he may cringe and whine, and attempt to lick the hand of the one who struck him, or he may lay bare his teeth, and spring for the throat of his assailant. Similar, or even more diverse results may follow an attack upon the man: he may run away, plead for mercy, return the attack with his fists or a stone or club, or he may draw a gun and kill his assailant. Or, again, he may run away only to return another day when he may deal with his opponent in a more effective way: he may "take the law into his own hands," or he may appeal to constituted authority for protection and retribution. The differences between the behavior of the ball on the one hand and that of the dog or man, on the other, are due entirely to the presence of consciousness, and of the ego in the latter two.

On this account it is clear that the mechanistic formula is inadequate or untrue, and must be replaced by some other which better expresses the facts. Two other formulæ have been suggested to express the patent relationship between the physical body and the ego.

1. There is the dualistic formula $B + E$, where B represents the body or physical aspect of the organism's personality, and E the non-physical ego or will.

2. There is the idealistic formula $E\ (b)$, where E represents the dominant character of the ego or will, and (b) the relation to it of the physical body.

These three formulæ put before us the three aspects of the great central problem of philosophy, the problem of *ultimate reality. We are entirely and far beyond the limits of science.* The data of physical science are entirely inadequate for its solution; we are in a realm where the conditions and conclusions cannot be found in the relations of molecules, atoms, electrons, radiant energy, heat, light, or electricity. No conclusions of science are sufficient for our purpose.

We must now consider the following questions:

1. Is the *materialistic* philosopher correct in his statement that the organism, or the human personality, if one wishes to limit the discussion to man, is in reality but the expression of the relations which exist among a mass of material units, atoms, electrons, or what not, which have an existence independent of consciousness, and which may produce that state as a function of their interactions? In short, should we adopt for the individual the first formula $B\ (e)$? Or

2. Is the *dualistic* philosopher correct in his assertion that human individuality is composed of two *coordinate* realities, the physical body and the non-physical ego, which we may not only distinguish in our thought, but which really are separate entities, more or less temporarily united or associated in the human organism? Should we therefore accept his formula, $B + E$? Or,

3. Is the *idealistic* philosopher correct in his contention that the individual is in reality a non-physical or *spiritual* entity, an ego associated with physical manifestations? Is the body of the organism an *ideal* one, *though none the less real*, a mechanism by means of which the ego operates? Is the true formula, therefore, $E\ (b)$?

These are questions which have occupied the attention and thought of philosophers and many men eminent in science for several hundred years. Some have adopted one conclusion, some another, but since the time of Berkeley (1685-1753) there has been a constantly increasing tendency to repudiate the materialistic assumption and to adopt the conclusion that "in ultimate analysis and in *reality* our world and the individual is spiritual." As Lloyd Morgan has remarked: "It was Berkeley who knocked the bottom out of materialism as a philosophy so that no amount of tinkering can make it again hold water."

To one who has not been trained to think deeply and correctly the external world seems to be made up only of those phenomena perceived by the senses. There is no idea that sense-perceptions may not be absolutely accurate. This "common sense" point of view seems to be entirely adequate for the ordinary situations with which he has to deal and there is at first no thought of anything below the surface of things. Later, the student learns to distinguish between an *internal* and an *external reality*, and he finally comes to ask, "How much can I know of external reality?" When this stage is reached, the student discovers that his knowledge of the "external" world comes to him only through the physical senses of touch, taste, smell, hearing, sight, etc. In other words, through the physiological functioning of the sense-organs and the psychological processes which go on in his brain he receives his "knowledge" of nature. This process involves three steps:

1. The *stimulus* (the object in the external world);

2. The *nerve disturbance* (caused by the stimulus);

3. The *sensation* or *sense-impression* (the result of the nerve disturbance).

By his study of chemistry and physics the student learns that "all the phenomena of the external world may be reduced to or expressed in terms of atoms or electrons in motion, rapidly in gases, less so in liquids and still less so in solids; that all chemical change involves the rearrangement of atoms and finally that all forms of energy depend on the rapid movement of atoms. Moreover, the physiologist assures him that these assertions hold true for the living as well as for the lifeless. Thus the physical (external) universe appears to be a universe of atoms or electrons in motion" (Neal).

So far the student is perfectly correct in his ideas and conclusions; he has arrived at the *scientific mechanistic interpretation* of the physical world, an interpretation established by scientific data and universally accepted by the modern world. "*Its validity as a scientific hypothesis stands unchallenged.* There is no reason whatever to believe that in principle it will ever be overthrown." But the sense of the correctness of this mechanistic principle sometimes becomes so strong that the student is tempted to carry it to unwarranted lengths. He applies the hypothesis to mental phenomena and concludes that consciousness is merely the result of the interaction of atoms or electrons when brought together in certain proportions and under certain conditions. In short, he goes beyond demonstrable facts of science into the realm of speculation, where the modern philosopher is not able to follow him. He concludes that the universe is in reality a universe of atoms and electrons unrelated to consciousness in any fundamental way. He thus steps, unconsciously perhaps, over the line between the realm of the mechanistic scientist into that of the materialistic philosopher. Let us see whether his conclusions are well taken and solidly supported by fact.

Primarily "the data of science are phenomena of consciousness. For anything to be outside of consciousness, therefore, is to be *unknown,* and hence outside of the field of science which deals with the known. To postulate an external world of atoms and electrons independent of—or outside of—consciousness is to postulate an *unknowable world—a metaphysical world.* It is a wholly erroneous notion that this conclusion of philosophy involves the denial of an external world— the permanent possibility of sensation." (Neal) Thus, "when human beings speak—that is, when we hear certain noises which we associate with ideas, and simultaneously see certain motions of lips and expressions of face—it is very difficult to suppose that what we hear is not the expression of a thought, as we know it would be if we emitted the same sounds. Of course similar things happen in dreams, where we are mistaken as to the existence of other people. But dreams are more or less suggested by what we call waking life, and are capable of being more or less accounted for on scientific principles if we assume that there is really a physical world. Thus every principle of simplicity urges us to adopt the natural view, that there really are objects other than our selves and our sense data which have an existence not dependent upon our perceiving them." (Russell, "The Problems of Philosophy," p. 37.)

"There is indeed (to the idealist not less than to the realist) an external world which is the cause of our ideas. But this *external* world of ours must be a world of *ideas*—that is, if it is like our ideas as we believe it is. *But if objects in this external world are like our ideas, then they must be ideas.* Therefore, either the real external world is a world of ideas—an outer world of mind which each of us may in a measure comprehend through experience, or—so far as it is external and real—it is wholly unknowable" (Royce, 92, *vide* Neal). That the world of science is withal a world of ideas has been appreciated by scientific thinkers scarcely less than by philosophers.

"Our one certainty is the existence of the mental world," wrote Huxley. "Ego is the only reality and everything else is Ego's idea," said Charles Sedgwick Minot, professor of embryology and dean of the Harvard Medical School. "The sole reality that we are able to discover in the world is mind," says Verworn, professor of physiology in the University of Jena, in his "General Physiology." "Our world is after all a world of individual consciousness and ideas," says Crampton, professor of zoology at Columbia University. "The field

THE PROBLEM OF ULTIMATE CAUSATION

of science is essentially the contents of the mind," says Karl Pearson, of Cambridge University (England) in his encyclopedic work, called "The Grammar of Science."

The dualistic postulate $(B + E)$ has little standing among philosophers, since it is well recognized that it is but a thinly disguised materialism, with its doctrine of epiphenomenalism, and all the arguments against philosophic materialism apply equally against it. Minot remarks of epiphenomenalism: "An epiphenomenon is something superimposed upon the actual phenomena having no causal relation to the further development of the process. There is no idea at all underneath the epiphenomenon hypothesis of consciousness. The hypothesis is simply an empty phrase, a subterfuge, which amounts to this: we can explain consciousness very easily by merely assuming that it does not require to be explained at all." W. MacDougall, in his book, "Body and Mind," p. 150, says: "Epiphenomenonism, though it may perhaps be consistent with the law of the conservation of energy, offends against a law that has a much stronger claim to universality, namely the law of causality itself; for it assumes that a physical process, say a molecular movement of the brain, *causes* a sensation, but does so *without* the cause passing over in any degree into the effect, without the cause spending itself in any degree in the production of the effect, namely, the sensation."

Consequently in our consideration of the probblem of individuality, we are compelled to make our choice between philosophical materialism and idealism, that is to say, between mind and matter (independent of mind) as the basis of individuality. "Our choice is to be made between a postulate which is philosophically disreputable and one which has been accepted by the great philosophers of recent times from Berkeley and Kant to Emerson, Royce and James; between the assumption of a wholly unknowable and metaphysical world and the indisputable assumption that our one surest reality is consciousness; between the Haeckelian riddle and the assumption that our world has moral and spiritual meaning; between a world in which the words and gestures of every individual "would have been just what they have been, the same empires would have arisen and fallen, the same masterpieces of music and poetry would have been produced, the same indications of friendship and affection would have been given in the absence of consciousness" (Lloyd Morgan), and the "common sense" view of the historian that human motives and purposes have affected the course of human events; between a fatalistic world of illusion, on the one hand, and a world in which choices are real and ideals count; between an assumption which renders untenable the great human ideas of God, freedom of the will, and immortality, and one which gives these unquestionable validity" (Neal).

That modern philosophy has repudiated the materialistic postulate is not surprising in the light of the considerations which we have presented.

THE PROBLEM OF ULTIMATE CAUSATION

Since the materialistic postulate is not only philosophically unsound and wholly unnecessary for any ends which the scientist has in view; since it is metaphysical, unscientific and irrational—wholly inconsistent with the lives of those who make it as Conklin contends ("Heredity and Environment in the Development of Man")—biologists are more and more becoming convinced that it must be rejected and that the idealistic assumption must be accepted in science as well as in modern philosophy. There must be the realization of "the indisputable truth that the laws of mechanics and motion themselves are in final analysis nothing else but laws of thought of the reasoning mind, and derive their first and only warrant from the higher reality of that mind" (D. G. Brinton, quoted by H. V. Neal).

The question now arises, "Is the doctrine of evolution inconsistent with the philosophical position here advanced and accepted?" More specifically the question may be raised as to the reconciliation of the idealistic philosophy with the doctrine of the evolution of the human race. These questions have been answered, *more Scottico,* by asking two others:

1. Is it possible for us to believe that a chaos has become a cosmos without the effective cooperation of a directive intelligence or will?

2. Is it possible to believe on rational grounds that a material universe *devoid of mind* has produced a mind capable of judging mechanism?

J. J. Putnam, in "Human Motives," raises

these questions to answer them in these words: "If this were true it would seem possible for a man to raise himself by his own boot-straps. But if it be impossible for mechanism (unguided by intelligence) to produce the mind of a person capable of judging mechanism, it is clear that mechanism has not been the only principle at work in the evolutionary process." Minot, already referred to, says in a paper published in *Science,* 1902: "It seems to me inconceivable that the evolution of animals should have taken place as it actually has taken place unless consciousness is a real factor and dominant. Accordingly I hold that it actually affects the vital processes. There is, in my judgment, no possibility of avoiding the conclusion that consciousness stands in immediate causal relations with physiological processes. To say this is to abide by the facts, as at present known to us, and with the facts our conceptions must be made to accord."

The whole trend of the doctrine of evolution is inescapably toward the point of view of the modern theologian when he says:

"Never yet has something come out of nothing. Never yet has order arisen out of confusion or light out of darkness as a result of anything other than personality. Force, law, life, and achievement carry the mind irresistibly to the supreme will, to the supreme life, to the personality of God. A universe teeming with mind, fired within and stamped without with intelligence is the attestation of the living God. God is the meaning of the universe.

"Behind all human achievement we see the creative spirit at work. Back of all achievement in literature we see the personality of Homer and Aeschylus, Dante, Goethe and Shakespeare. Behind the achievements of the race in art we see the personality of Praxiteles, Raphael and Michael Angelo. For the entire high achievement of the race there is no explanation but the creative spirit of human personality. In our contemplation of nature and in our attempt to comprehend it we need to carry with us the sense of creation. The universe is the supreme achievement. Behind this achievement is the infinite soul and as our human world is a living and expanding achievement, we must conclude that within it is the creative spirit of God." (G. A. Gordon, "The Appeal to Cæsar," in the *Congregationalist*, Vol. 95. 1910.)

Thus we may discern with Tennyson in the progress of evolution

> "One God, one law, one element,
> And one far-off divine event
> To which the whole creation moves."

CHAPTER X

THE ORIGIN OF THE INDIVIDUAL
VERSUS THE ORIGIN OF THE
SPECIES

ONCE upon a time in the days when knighthood was in flower, two yokels were walking along a road engaged in friendly conversation. By and by as their gaze ran along the way in front they saw a handsomely equipped knight approaching on horseback. He was clad in a coat-of-mail, and carried his lance in his right hand, while on his left arm he bore his shield. As he came near, the two yokels stepped to opposite sides of the road to allow him to pass between them. Bareheaded, with hats in hand, they stood at respectful attention while he rode by without so much as a glance in their direction. Directly the two continued their walk and naturally fell to discussing the knight, his appearance, his steed, and his accoutrement. Loud were their praises of his various articles of equipment, until one remarked upon the beautiful *white* shield which he bore upon his arm. The other immediately exclaimed: "White! You fool! That was no white shield—it was black as jet!" "You're the fool!" replied the first, "I tell you it was white; your eyes were blinded by the sun, if it looked black to you!" So the wordy contest grew more and more heated and acrimonious until at last one passed that short ugly word that brought on the blow. Fists flew thick and fast, eyes became black and noses bloody. At last while pommelling each other on the ground, neither willing to concede any measure of truth in the other's opinion, one of their friends came along, and, seeing the fight, inquired the cause. As the one explained that the shield was white, while the second was equally sure that it was black, the quarrel was renewed and the fight was about to begin again, when the mutual friend had a happy thought. "Come, come, fellows!" he said, "What is the use of quarreling and fighting over such an absurd thing? Don't you see that, since one of you says that the shield is white, while the other is equally sure that it is black, the shield must be gray?"

This compromise solution of their difficulty appealed to the illiterate yokels, who made up and continued their journey on friendly terms once more. They had not gone far on their way when the sound of a horseman approaching them from the rear caused them both to turn their heads, only to see the same knight retracing the road he had so recently travelled in the opposite direction. Once again the two yokels stood at either side of the road in an outward attitude of respect, though inwardly each was resolved to look more particularly at the shield to make sure that he had been right about its color. To their astonishment, the one who had formerly so stoutly asserted the blackness of the shield now perceived its snowy whiteness, while the other, who had previously contended even to his own hurt that the shield was white, now discovered it to have the hue of the darkest midnight! Each was now so bent on apology to his friend for having before disputed his word, that they again came near to blows: but luckily at this point a turn in the road brought them within sight of a public inn, at which the knight was alighting.

As he did so he passed his shield over to his squire, who turned, as the yokels approached, in such a way that they could plainly see first the one side and then the other of the shield,. when lo! they saw that it was white on one side and black on the other! They had both been right, absolutely right in their assertions as to the color each had seen; they had both been wrong in refusing to consider the matter from the other's point of view. Furthermore, the one individual who had been wholly wrong in the matter was the friendly peacemaker who had sought by his shallow thinking to effect a compromise on *gray* as the color of the shield. The shield was both *black and white,* but not at any time *gray.*

This parable teaches a fundamental truth which is founded upon an abundance of human experience, namely, that when a question of fact arises over which men debate long and heatedly, and for which both sides are willing to and do make great personal sacrifices to establish their respective positions, the truth is usually to be found partly on both sides, which may be reconciled, but not by a compromise which is false to both. Moreover, no position wholly in error can long withstand the assaults made upon it; the longer the debate the surer is it that there is truth upon both sides, perhaps not unmingled with error, which must be refined away, but it is an assuring fact that the *"truth is mighty and will prevail."*

Now, the conflict of opinion between science and theology as to the method of creation is just such a matter as this. For many years, the conflict has been waged with varying fortunes as one doughty champion has faced another; most fiercely when some materialist, like Haeckel, has wielded the sword on the side of science and some idealist has championed the cause of the church. No *compromise* of views in this cause can come any nearer the truth than did the third yokel in our parable. The materialist and the theologian have generally each been right in the assertion of the truth as he saw it, and both have been equally wrong in refusing to see the truth of their opponents. The way of reconciliation, not of compromise, lies in the candid and open-minded examination of both sides to determine wherein each is right, and wherein each is wrong. When this is done it will be found that the partial truth of each fits into that of the other to make the *whole* truth well-rounded and complete.

The origin of the individual as well as of the species may be explained on any one of three different theories. Two of these are mutually nullifying—if one is wholly right then the other is wholly wrong. But the third theory finds truth in both and combines it in such a way as to harmonize and reconcile the partial truths into a logical and reasonable whole, which is then perceived by the unprejudiced investigator to be a grander and nobler view than either of the others. Thus, as LeConte long ago pointed out, there are three theories of individual origin current in the minds of men. The first is that taught by many pious but uninformed parents to their children, namely, that they are made in some miraculous way directly by the Creator. "God made us," is the reply so frequently heard to the child's eager questioning about his origin. The second is the thought of the untaught street-gamin, or of Topsy, who said: "I was not made at all; I just growed." Or, in the language of the materialist, the individual is the product of resident forces in the egg. The third answer is that of most intelligent Christians, that *God made us through a natural process*. To one who has observed directly the development of the living egg, from its relatively simple and apparently unorganized condition into the complex individual which it gradually becomes, the natural processes of cell-multiplication, differentiation, unequal growth of parts, etc, all are apparent enough. *It grows.* But, the thoughtful observer of the phenomenon cannot help being impressed by the fact that the mechanical forces observed do not constitute the *ultimate* explanation of the phenomenon. The egg is moulded as by the hand of an invisible potter. The ultimate creative energy of the universe, God himself, is revealed in the process.

Observe that this third conclusion combines and reconciles the partial truths of both the other theories. It is therefore more reasonable than either of them. It harmonizes them into a philosophically sound position that rests on the scientific evidence of the embryologist and the religious experience of the theologian. It is a conclusion that cannot be successfully assailed from any standpoint.

In like manner, one can account for the origin of species on three exactly analogous theories. The first is that so widely held by the literalistically orthodox clergymen and laymen alike who assert that species were made out of hand by the Creator without the operation of any natural process. That God spoke a word and the dust of the earth became a living organism. It is the theory of Special Creation adopted as the orthodox doctrine of the Roman Catholic Church and taken over into Protestant theology bodily from the same source. The second theory is that of the materialist who asserts that there was no creation at all; that species were derived from non-living matter through a happy concatenation of circumstances. That "chance" brought together certain inorganic elements in a certain relationship and that "life" is the peculiar manifestation of the interactions of the atoms or electrons of those elements. This theory asserts the sufficiency of the

THE INDIVIDUAL VERSUS THE SPECIES

resident forces of nature to produce all organisms from the simplest monad up to man. "Species," in the language of Topsy, "just growed." The third theory is that of the theistic evolutionist, who asserts that *species were created by a process of evolution;* that the Creative Intelligence directed the processes of nature in a way so far unknown to the physicist and chemist. On this view *species were made,* but not in such a way as to preclude all further growth and development. Quoting from LeConte: "The first asserts divine agency, but denies natural process; the second asserts the natural process, but denies divine agency; the third asserts divine agency by natural process. Of the first two, observe, both are right and both wrong; each view is right in what it asserts, and wrong in what it denies—each is right from its own point of view, but wrong in excluding the other point of view. The third is the only true rational solution, for it includes, combines, and reconciles the other two; showing wherein each is right and wherein wrong. It is the combination of the two partial truths, and the elimination of the partial errors. But let us not fail to do perfect justice. The first two views of origin, whether of the individual or of the species, are indeed both partly wrong as well as partly right; but the view of the pious child or of the Christian contains by far the more essential truth. Of the two sides of the shield, theirs is at least the whiter and more beautiful.

"But, alas! the great bar to a speedy settlement of this question and the adoption of a rational philosophy is not in the head, but in the heart—is not in the reason, but in pride of opinion, self-conceit, dogmatism. The rarest of all gifts is a truly tolerant, rational spirit. In all our gettings let us get this, for it alone is true wisdom. But we must not imagine that all the dogmatism is on one side, and that the theological. Many seem to think that theology has a "presumptive right" to dogmatism. If so, the modern materialistic science has "jumped the claim." Dogmatism has its roots deep-bedded in the human heart. It showed itself first in the domain of theology, because there was the seat of power. In modern times it has gone over to the side of science, because here now is the place of power and fashion. There are two dogmatisms, both equally opposed to the true rational spirit, viz., the old theological and the new scientific. The old clings fondly to old things, only because they are old; the new grasps eagerly after new things, only because they are new. True wisdom and true philosophy, on the contrary, tries all things both old and new, and holds fast only to that which is good and true. The new dogmatism taunts the old for credulity and superstition; the old reproaches the new for levity and skepticism. But true wisdom perceives that they are both equally credulous and equally skeptical. The old is credulous of old ideas and skeptical of new; the new is skeptical of old ideas and credulous of new. Both deserve the unsparing rebuke of all right-minded men. The appropriate rebuke for the old dogmatism has been already put into the mouth of

The Individual Versus the Species

Job in the form of the bitter sneer: "No doubt ye are the people, and wisdom shall die with you." The appropriate rebuke for the new dogmatism though not put into the mouth of any ancient prophet, ought to be uttered—I will undertake to utter it here. I would say to these modern materialists: "No doubt ye are the men, and wisdom and true philosophy were born with you." (LeConte, "Evolution," 2nd ed., 1897.)

A further, shorter quotation from Le Conte sums up the conclusion here set forth so well that we cannot forbear to give it. He says:

"The process and the law of evolution does not differ in its relation to materialism from all other processes and laws of nature. If the sustentation of the universe by the law of gravitation does not disturb our belief in God as the sustainer of the universe, there is no reason why the origin of the universe by the law of evolution should disturb our faith in God as the creator of the universe. If the law of gravitation be regarded as the Divine mode of sustentation, there is no reason why we should not regard the law of evolution as the Divine process of creation. It is evident that if evolution be materialism, then is gravitation also materialism; then is every law of nature and all science materialism. If there be any difference at all, it consists only in this: that . . . here is the last line of defense of the supporters of supernaturalism in the realm of nature."

It has always seemed strange to the present author that those who accept the "natural" origin of the individual as a demonstrated fact of nature and do not find it disturbing to their theological beliefs, should consider the "natural" origin of species so destructive. It is certainly, *a priori*, a much more wonderful fact that the individual in a few short years, not to say months, literally *evolves* from a simple spherical cell only 1-120th of an inch in diameter, with absolutely none of the organs or parts of the adult, into a *man* with all his wonderful complexity of organization, and his ability to think, to reason, and to will, than that a species has been produced by evolution through millions of years from a simpler beginning. If God can and does by natural processes create the individual man in the length of time required for his prenatal development, his infancy and his youth, why think it strange, or belittling of His power and wisdom, to find that He took millions of years in developing organic creation up to the point where man became a rational spirit —the true image of his Maker?

CHAPTER XI

WHAT AND WHERE IS GOD?

IT has been our purpose to show that every great scientific discovery has had its influence on the current or traditional philosophy and religion. In this respect the doctrine of evolution is no different from the law of gravitation, the discovery of the great antiquity of the earth and of man, or the heliocentric theory of the solar system. It simply carries the process logically a step farther and forces the issue, so that it can be no longer compromised nor evaded. The traditional view of God and His relation to nature and to man has the force of hoary age upon it; it has the stamp of approval of high ecclesiastical authority; to maintain their belief in it, martyrs have suffered torture on the rack, crucifixion on the cross, or death at the stake.

Philosophically, there have been several answers made to the question, What and where is God? One of these is that of materialism which denies His existence at all. Since we have already shown that materialism is philosophically unsound, it is not necessary to discuss its position further. Among those, however, who reject the atheism of the materialist, there is and has been a considerable variation of opinion in regard to the spiritualistic principle on which must rest all the cosmic phenomena. At various times and in the minds of various people the opinions have taken the form (1) of *polytheism,* (2) of *pantheism,* (3) of *deism,* and (4) of *theism.*

Polytheism, as the name implies, is the primitive, superstitious belief in many gods. At the present time it has no philosophical standing and is found only in the superstition of the untutored savage or barbarian who sees a god of good or evil intent in every object and phenomenon of nature. This theory is the product of man's groping in the darkness of ignorance for an explanation of the great mysteries which surround him and in relation to which he feels himself to have a deep concern. A further consideration of polytheism is not necessary for our purpose.

Pantheism is a theory which looks upon the universe as the sole and complete manifestation of God. *"God is all and all is God"* is the cry of the pantheist. It is an interesting fact that pantheism has appealed more strongly to those of poetic vision than to those more philosophically inclined. The English poet, Wordsworth, in his *Lines Composed Above Tintern Abbey,* gives what Hibben characterizes as a "most profound and subtle expression of pantheistic interpretation," in these lines:

"For I have learned
To look on nature, not as in the hour
Of thoughtless youth; but hearing oftentimes

What and Where is God?

> The still, sad music of humanity,
> Nor harsh, nor grating, though of ample power
> To chasten and subdue. And I have felt
> A presence that disturbs me with the joy
> Of elevated thoughts: a sense sublime
> Of something far more deeply interfused,
> Whose dwelling is the light of setting suns,
> And the round ocean, and the living air,
> And the blue sky, and in the mind of man:
> A motion and a spirit that impels
> All thinking things, all objects of all thought,
> And rolls through all things."

The renowned poet, Goethe, gives a clear statement of this pantheistic belief in these words:

"What were a God who only gave the world a push from without, or let it spin around His finger? I look for a God who moves the world from within, who fosters nature in Himself, Himself in nature, so that naught of all that lives and moves and has its being in Him ever forgets His force or His spirit."

Hibben ("Problems of Philosophy," p. 70) points out the generally recognized fact that

"Pantheism takes two forms, which do not differ, however, fundamentally. The one identifies God completely with the world of being, coming to His highest manifestation in the consciousness of man. From the lowest to the highest, from the simplest to the most complex forms of this manifestation, all is God. The other view emphasizes the divine as the only reality and reduces the facts of existence to a mere appearance, the shadowy semblance of reality. While the former view denies all difference between God and the world, including man, the latter insists that the seeming difference must be regarded as a mental illusion, having no basis in reality. In either case, God's immanence is magnified to the exclusion of His transcendence. It is a convenient philosophy, the reference of everything to God; it unties many hard knots, it cuts in twain many more."

Deism is the belief of the usual orthodox Christian. It is philosophically but "a refined form of polytheism." For the many gods of the polytheist, it simply substitutes one god, or rather it combines and fuses into one the many gods of polytheism. It attributes to its one God the same attributes which, in polytheism, are parcelled out to the many. "The God of the deist is an "enlarged man," an artificer rather than a creator; the world is regarded as a stupendous mechanism rather than a manifestation of the life of the supreme Being" (Hibben). This is the traditional view of God which looks upon Him as a great master mechanic who upon an occasion long ago constructed the huge machine of the universe and all that is within it, like a great clock made up of wheels (matter) and weights or springs (energy), so perfectly constructed, so adequately adjusted in all its parts, that having once been set going it could run on through the allotted period of time with no further need of direction or attention from the Maker. And then having accomplished this great work out of hand, the Maker *rested*.

Or, the traditional view may be likened unto that of the head of a great business enterprise who has so organized his affairs, who has employed such competent assistants that he no longer needs to devote his time and attention to the business, but is able to enjoy his golf, his hunting or fishing, his travel abroad, perfectly assured that the business will go on without interruption in his absence. His subordinates are trained and perform their duties without intervention on his part, unless perchance matters do not always go along quite so smoothly. Little annoyances arise, friction occurs, accidents happen, and the subordinates appeal to the absent chief by telegraph or by telephone, asking for further direction, for help and guidance in the complications that have arisen to perplex and annoy them. More or less directly the merchant chief has to adjust matters, make changes here and there in his organization, perhaps eliminate parts that do not function properly, or introduce new blood into the staff, or new stock on the shelves. But in the main things go pretty much in routine ways. Now and then the merchant may even have to return in person to perform the duties that no subordinate is capable of undertaking; reorganization must be made; expansion or enlargement of the field of operations must be provided for; and then he may go away for another period of rest or travel, subject to summons at any time by post or telegraph.

Just as pantheism emphasizes the immanence of God to the exclusion of His transcendence, so deism emphasizes the transcendence of God to the exclusion of His immanence. They are therefore mutually exclusive and contradictory. Pantheism and materialism, the former by elevating nature up to God, the latter by degrading God down to an identity with nature, finally merge indistinguishably into each other. There is therefore a mutual exclusion or contradiction between deism on the one hand and pantheism and materialism on the other.

Theism at once combines and reconciles the truth in so far as it finds expression in deism and pantheism; it takes their partial truths, eliminates their errors, and arrives at a view of God that is the grandest and noblest possible to the human mind. Theism "takes exception, not to that which pantheism asserts, but to that which pantheism denies, or ignores, namely, the transcendence of God" (Hibben). "It is differentiated from deism in that it insists upon the sustaining and operating presence of God in all phenomena of the universe. Theism denies the possibility of an "absentee God." It differs, however, on the other hand, from pantheism in affirming the existence of a real distinction between God and his works, between the Creator and the creature, especially as this distinction is emphasized in the consciousness of a self which refuses to be absorbed in the great All of pantheism. Thus theism is an attempt to synthesize within a higher unity the two opposed

WHAT AND WHERE IS GOD?

ideas of transcendence and immanence, and which regards God as manifesting Himself in and through His works, and yet as a personality, distinct from them" (Hibben).

While the poets have generally inclined to the purely pantheistic view, the philosophizing scientists have often felt the force of the materialistic hypothesis. To them it has seemed that matter and energy must always have existed; that they could have had no creation, since the production of something out of nothing is contrary to all experience, and hence there could have been no creator. Matter and energy being indestructible will, therefore, have no end. Their existence is from the infinity of past time to the infinity of future time. The materialist asserts furthermore that not only are they thus eternal but by themselves are able to and have accomplished the production of all the forms of animate and inanimate nature. Resident forces account for all the phenomena of the universe from electron to reason, from the universal ether to human consciousness, from the harmony of the spheres to the moral sense in man. Since, on this view, the universe is infinite both in time and space, and since there is no directing agency in it but blind chance and the law of necessity, there is not only no god but no room nor need of one.

The orthodox deistic view and this are mutually antagonistic and mutually exclusive. Scientific research and discovery have more and more removed the phenomena of nature from the operation of the traditional view of the Creator's handiwork, until it would appear at times, as many have thought, that materialism is about to capture the whole realm of nature. One by one the traditional ideas of the relation of the earth to the sun and other planets, of the age of the earth and of man, of the origin of inanimate and animate objects, have had to give way to the discoveries of science until it seemed as though the whole foundation of our philosophical and religious edifice was slipping away like a house built upon the sand. Evolution is simply the latest of these great discoveries of science. To many good people it has seemed that those which went before had resulted only in the surrender of more or less unimportant outworks, had compelled strategic retreats from terrain that should never have been occupied, but this latest attack would seem to compel the falling back to an entirely new position, to the surrender of the very citadel which had been our shelter in all the centuries past, to the vanquishment of all that is highest, holiest, and most worth while in life, and the annihilation of all our fondest hopes for the future.

As LeConte long ago pointed out, when the law of gravitation became the accepted view, it was felt that while the *course* of nature might be explained as due to resident forces, there still remained the *origin* of things as inexplicable on any such grounds. God's hand appeared necessary to fashion and to form every new appearance of matter or energy, but evolution seemed to take

WHAT AND WHERE IS GOD?

away even this necessity. Resident forces *seemed* sufficient to account for *origins* as well as *courses*. Natural law operated here as elsewhere. Just as the old view that God supports the world in the hollow of His hand gave way to the view that the laws of attraction and repulsion were sufficient to account for the earth's journey through space, so it seemed that here the old view that God made all things should have to give way to Topsy's view that they "merely grew." Evolution then forces the issue—either nature is all sufficient and needs no God, or else the traditional view is utterly inadequate.

The dilemma is inescapable—it must be resolutely faced. The sooner theologians realize the situation and resolutely face the problem, the better it will be for the world. No attempt to discredit the results of science will avail. Day by day those results are rendered more substantial and undeniable. More and more are these results of science entering into the philosophy of the people. It is futile to close our eyes to the real situation. It is criminal to refuse to see it as it is. So long as there are those who are ignorant of scientific discovery, so long will there be those who are content with traditional views, but every day finds more and more of our young people confronted with the irrefutable facts of science which are irreconcilable with traditional theological dogma. The result is rampant materialism, for which theology is responsible and not science, for it is theology which has so often refused to square its teaching with the facts. Practically, this condition is emptying both pulpits and pews. "According to Dr. Robert L. Kelley, secretary of the Council of Church Boards of Education, fully five thousand Protestant pulpits are now vacant in this country, and another five thousand will need ministers next year. To meet this demand the seminaries graduated in June (1921) only 1,600 students, and not all of these can be counted on for ministerial service.

"While colleges, universities and other professional schools are crowded beyond precedent, the theological seminaries, with significant exceptions, are losing disastrously. Attendance at Episcopalian seminaries decreased from 463 in 1916 to 193 in 1920. In Presbyterian seminaries it decreased from 1188 in 1916 to 695 in 1921; in Methodist seminaries from 1226 in 1916 to 976, and in Congregational seminaries from 499 in 1910 to 255 in 1921.

"Explanations of these losses which are coming from seminary authorities and ministers are superficial and unconvincing. Most of them allege the war and its effects. That this theory is of little value appears from contrasting Roman Catholic gains. Attendance at Roman Catholic seminaries (which stand upon the affirmation of ecclesiastical authority) has been and is gaining. There is more than a hint in this fact of what some of the real causes at work are. A hint of other and different but cooperating causes is given in the prosperity of the Union Theological Seminary, which a reactionary element in the Presbyterian body once tried to put out of business. Maintaining a university connection, high standards of up-to-date scholarship, and a liberal attitude, Union Seminary is attracting year by year an increasing number of well-prepared and serious-minded students, worthy to be compared in ability with the young men who go into law, medicine, engineering, and other professions that demand intelligence and knowledge." (Franklin H. Giddings, in *The Independent,* August 20, 1921, p. 67.)

In this same article Professor Giddings, whose well known abilities and attainments entitle him to speak with authority, and compel respectful attention, clarifies his diagnosis still further in these words:

"It would be a waste of energy at this late day to review the obstinacy with which Protestant theologians, rejecting authoritative formulations of belief from Rome, and professing liberty to interpret the Scriptures under accountability to the individual conscience, nevertheless resisted knowledge. They not only did not inform themselves . . . ; but also they did their best to keep scientific facts from inquisitive youth by branding indispensable books as dangerous or worse. Whether or not this was sin, it was an absurdity that queered Protestant theology.

"Truth is either authoritatively declared in doctrine and interpretations that should be accepted without question, or it is arrived at through untrammeled investigation. Authority is either a creative source which "makes good," or it is derived from a creative source by grant or concession. If derived, it necessarily is or becomes traditional. Traditional authority, proclaimed by historical institutions still functioning, cannot be rejected without asserting the right to question, to deny, and to investigate. When, therefore, Protestantism, having rejected the authority of Rome, attempted to discredit inductive science and historical scholarship, it stultified itself. Young men of parts were not slow to see the implications. Strongly religious natures that were reverential toward tradition, began to drift towards Rome. Investigating minds turned to inductive science or to business. Exceptionally strong men of both types were lost to the Protestant pulpit."

What holds true for the pulpit also applies to the pew. The layman was no less able to perceive the lameness of the theology passed out to him Sunday by Sunday. Attendance and interest in the church became perfunctory; the religious nature of the people more and more found its expression in deeds of charity. It is a fact that puzzles many a minister that in an age when materialism and disregard for the church seem so rampant, nevertheless the spirit of charity never was so marked. Men who never darken a church door spend liberally of time, strength, and money to relieve the sufferings of the poverty-stricken, the sick and the afflicted. The Red Cross and the Salvation Army, as well as Associated Charity organizations, are supported as never before, while the churches are hard put to it to make ends meet with their budgets.

The salvation of the world depends upon the discovery of the ground where the imperishable truths of both science and religion may be found to dovetail together into a complete and harmonious whole. This cannot be accomplished with traditional orthodox theology with its *deistic* view of God. There must be a change of base. The forces of religion must make their stand upon fundamental truths, and must discard the unnecessary chaff with which they have been accustomed to inclose the kernel of truth. Remembering the parable of the shield, it is clear that the path is one of reconciliation and not of compromise. The materialistic view is correct in its assertion of the role of resident forces in carrying on the course of nature, but wrong in its denial of a Conscious Agency in whose employ they are. The traditional view of theology is correct in its assertion of the Consciousness that directs all things but wrong in its denial to that Being of the *means* of *natural law*. Each is correct in its positive facts but wrong in its denial of the facts on the other side. The idea of creation by Divine Will without natural process is just as contrary to the facts as revealed by science, as is the opposite materialistic view of creation by natural processes without Divine Will. On the theistic view, as set forth above, we may exclaim with LeConte, how beautifully both these mutually antagonistic and mutually exclusive views become harmonized or reconciled—not compromised—upon the basis of *creation by Divine Will through natural process*. So the materialistic idea of a universe without a God of any kind save the many gods of resident forces is just as impossible as the traditional notion of the absentee landlord, of the infinite, yet how manlike, deity who lives away from the objects of His creation.

Science drives us to the conclusion that either there is no worshipful God at all, or else He is one who is much closer to nature and operates in a more direct way than the traditional view allows. He is at once both an immanent and a transcendental Being. All the mighty works of nature proclaim Him to be endowed with *conscious intelligence*. The operation of the law of evolution proves that He is *now, as ever,* consciously working out the universal plan which was with Him from the beginning, a plan which finds its present culmination in man. He is *literally,* not figuratively, in the words of the Apostle Paul, *"Him in whom we (and all things) live and move and have our being."* With materialism or pantheism, "to equate God with the universe without remainder, exhausts His being and manifestly limits Him to a definite comprehension within finite bounds. He is no longer the Eternal, the Infinite One! God is in nature, and yet He is more than nature. . . . In this distinction lies the essence of the theistic contention. Moreover, the absorption of all things in God reduces man's personality to zero. This meets with a very determined protest from our self-asserting consciousness, which refuses to be merged

WHAT AND WHERE IS GOD?

in the universal All. In the relations between God and man, as in the relations between God and the world, it is still possible to hold that God manifests Himself to man in the still small voice within, and yet that man himself is more than a manifestation of God. There is a revelation of God to man in the light of reason, in the voice of conscience, and in the inspiration of the truth, yet it is a revelation *to* man; the self receives, the self is moved, the self is preserved in its integrity as the self, the man, and not as God" (Hibben). Or, as Martineau says ("A Study of Religion," vol. II, p. 180): "If truth, if righteousness, if love and faith, are all an influx of foreign light, the endowments, in virtue of which we are susceptible of them, are mere passive and recipient organs on to which they are delivered, and we have no agency of our own. But a *reason* that does no thinking for itself, a *conscience* that flings aside no temptation and springs to no duty, *affection* that toils in no chosen service of love, a *religious sentiment* that waits for such faith as may come into it, simply negative their own functions and disappear."

The immanence of God without His simultaneous transcendence is unthinkable on the theistic postulates. But the one is as necessary as the other. We cannot avoid the belief in His immanence; we cannot conceive Him as one who long ago and once for all, enacted laws and created matter and energy, worlds and animate beings, and then *rested* from His labors. His mind is constantly engaged and the phenomena of nature are the *objectified* results of His thinking and planning. The forces of nature are but the objectified forms of His divine energy. It is on this account that the world of matter and motion is a "real" world; it has an existence of which we are conscious, it has a permanence despite its constant flux, because it is the manifestation of the eternal permanence of its Creator. It obeys the "laws of nature," which are regular and orderly because they are the expression of the absolute logic of His intellectual processes. He is a God of law and order. In their investigations of natural phenomena, scientists are, in the words of Agassiz, engaged in thinking the Creator's thoughts after Him. Thus is seen the significance of LeConte's statement that "the law of gravitation is the divine method of sustentation; the law of evolution, the divine method of creation."

Our consideration of the nature of God brings us back to and confirms our idealistic philosophy, as set forth in a preceding chapter. It reaffirms the notion that "there is no ultimate efficient force but *spirit,* and no really *independent* existence except God." Further, while philosophical pantheism and materialism dissipate all our hopes of personal relations with God, the theistic view, here set forth and accepted, preserves and deepens these hopes. It gives ground for the most circumspect morality; we can no longer, like Adam, hope to hide away from the sight of God when He calls. The "all-seeing eye" is no far distant object that may perchance overlook our misdeeds.

WHAT AND WHERE IS GOD?

"Speak to Him thou for He hears, and Spirit
    with Spirit can meet—
Closer is He than breathing, and nearer than
    hands and feet."

CHAPTER XII

EVOLUTION AND GENESIS

IT is frequently stated that one cannot be an evolutionist and hold to his belief in the Bible as a revelation from God. The supposed antithesis between the currently accepted account of creation as given in Genesis and the doctrine of the derivation of species by descent with modification has been affirmed on the one hand by the atheistic materialists who are opposed to all forms of religious belief, and on the other hand by those who seek to uphold the traditional theology. That the former should have taken this position, is easy to understand; that the latter could not foresee the ultimate effect upon thousands of truly religious souls is hard to understand in the light of the previous conflicts between science and theology. But perhaps the real explanation lies, as we have already intimated, in the fact that the conflict is one between a new scientific discovery and the ignorance inherited from past generations.

The real question at issue with reference to the Book of Genesis, is that of the value and place of the Old Testament in Christian life and thought. The vast amount of discussion concerning it now appearing in various church papers indicates that it is one of the most vital and burning questions of the day. But this is only the experience of Christendom repeated again and again, for, as Frederick D. Kershner remarks in "The Restoration Movement":[1]

"Perhaps there is no field in which mistaken thinking has caused more harmful results than is true of the study of the Old Testament. The human race has suffered incalculably because of erroneous views at this point. Old Testament ideals, uncorrected by the teaching of the New Testament, are largely responsible for the many blots upon the history of Christian peoples and nations. A few illustrations only are: (1) Church persecution, (2) bigoted opposition to progress, (3) the whole history of witch-craft, (4) medieval and modern militarism, (5) the defense of slavery, (6) false conceptions of the Christian ordinances and doctrines. . . . The necessities of the case made it impossible for the full glory of the Divine Word for man to be revealed all at once, just as we do not teach little children all that grown-up people are taught. The Old Testament was intended for the childhood of humanity. It is a collection of books written at different times, under different circumstances and by different persons. It is utterly out of the question to quote every passage in it as of equal authority for men and women today. The only way to get at its real meaning and value is by studying the setting of the different books, observing carefully their nature and pur-

[1] The Standard Publishing Co., Cincinnati.

pose, and then applying the truths they contain in the light of the later revelation made through Jesus Christ. . . . The Old Testament, as the author of the Epistle to the Hebrews plainly shows, has been fulfilled, and in the place of the old will, or covenant, we have the new. Of course, any one familiar with law knows that an older will is always superseded by one of later date. Under such circumstances the older will is annulled. This does not mean that the old may not contain much that is true and much that is valuable and perhaps indispensable for its time, but it does mean that something better and later has taken its place for present purposes.

"It is obvious in view of the facts already stated, that to use the Old Testament as a substitute for the New is to commit a grievous error. It is the sort of error which led people to justify slavery by appealing to the law of Moses, and to hang and burn innocent people under the delusion that they were witches, because the Mosaic law said: "Thou shalt not permit a witch to live." The same kind of logic justifies the indiscriminate slaughter of non-combatants today by appealing to the killing of the Canaanites or the Amalekites by the people of Israel."

The same author further says in regard to the different methods of scriptural interpretation: The legalistic "method of interpretation is the one followed by those who insist upon the letter of the Word, without seeking first for the spirit of it. The old Pharisees were the special advocates of this view. Jesus combatted it constantly, saying upon a certain memorable occasion that the letter killeth, but the spirit giveth life. The legalist wants to obey every jot and tittle of the law, but in his slavish devotion to the text he almost invariably misses its real meaning. Legalism is the direct opposite of rationalism, and is just as far away from the truth. The two extremes of rationalism and legalism were exemplified in the time of Christ in the teaching of the Sadducees and the Pharisees. The former were the rationalists of their day, and the latter the legalists. Both positions were wrong, and both are equally condemned in the New Testament. There are many modern legalists, and not a few of them are in the Protestant churches. Wherever they are found, there will also be found a narrow, bigoted, uncharitable and formalistic type of religion. Legalism kills the life and leaves only the empty shell of Christianity. It blights the fairest flowering of the soul and drives out all of the finest graces of the Christian life. It is one of the greatest foes of genuine Christianity. The Scriptures themselves lay down the correct method by which they are to be interpreted. Jesus, in His use of the Old Testament, always strove to get at the principle involved regardless of the letter, and to proclaim supreme loyalty to that principle. He struck out boldly on the Sabbath-day question, and incurred the hostility of the Pharisees because He insisted upon the spirit, rather than the letter, of the law. He condemned the skeptical rationalism of the Sadducees no less than the narrow legalism of the rival party in Judaism. Paul followed the same line of procedure, although technically a Pharisee, in his thinking. The principle of interpretation which is involved is perfectly clear. The Scriptures are not to be deified. Their value lies solely in the message which they convey. They are the bearer of certain great truths and ideals, and it is these truths and ideals which are of supreme value, rather than the words which are used to convey them to the minds of others. The Bible is not intended to enslave the intellect, but, rather, to set it free. The whole question is one of the utmost life and freedom versus formalism on the one side and destructive rationalism on the other."

We have quoted thus at length from a theologian generally recognized among those of his own communion as "strictly orthodox" and from his book issued by the publishing house of the most conservative group of that communion, because it expresses exactly the principle of interpretation which we wish to apply to the Book of Genesis. Furthermore, as we have attempted to set forth above, his method is philosophically correct, in that it accepts the truth found partly in two extremes and rejects the error into which each has fallen.

The purpose of the author of Genesis and the relation of the Biblical account of creation to the doctrine of evolution has never, in the opinion of the present writer, been better and more clearly stated than by Fairhurst, a man who, strange to

Evolution and Christian Faith

say, utterly and entirely misapprehends and misunderstands the doctrine of evolution and its implications. In his book, "Organic Evolution Considered," pp. 346-348, he says:

"The cosmogony in Genesis is very general. It is an outline painted with a few bold strokes. It was given to a people who were in the infancy of civilization, the masses of whom were ignorant and illiterate. A complete history of creation, as it occurred through the long geological ages, would have been useless to them. They could not have understood it because of its length and complexity, and because they were totally ignorant of the facts on which the geological account must be based. If it had been fully written for them, it would have been bewildering. What object could have been accomplished by telling that people that trilobites and brachiopods abounded in the Silurian; that fishes of many kinds were very numerous in the Devonian; that labyrinthodonts basked in the sunshine on the shores of Carboniferous swamps; that mighty frogs croaked in the Triassic; that the marsupial, greatest great, great, etc., grandfather of the opossum, was then engaged in his craft of robbing the nests of the long-tailed archæopteryx; that the zeuglodon sported in the Gulf of Mexico, in the Eocene; that three and four-toed horses of various kinds played baseball with boulders in the Rocky Mountain region, thus ridding themselves of their surplus toes, during the Tertiary; that bears, tigers, and lions of huge size fought each other, like the Kilkenny cats, in

England during the same period; that monkeys chased each other up and down the trees and played "hide and seek" in the forests of the Pliocene; and that, by accident or otherwise, the anthropomorphous, gorilla-like ape lost his tail and took to intellectual and moral habits, so that sometime during the Quaternary Period he became Adam?

"All these things, with a great multitude of similar facts, which can hardly be numbered, are of interest to the geologist and the evolutionist with their knowledge of modern science, but to the people of the time of Moses it would have been unprofitable reading. The cosmogony of Genesis had an infinitely higher and nobler aim than the teaching of the long list of incomprehensible facts contained in the geological record. It was given to impress upon the minds of that people and of the world, the fact of the existence of the one omnipotent, omniscient, righteous God as the creator of all things, and to whom all men are responsible for their conduct. This teaching of Monotheism came upon the infant race as a revelation, as a flash from Heaven, more marvelous than the creation of physical things. It was the one great fact that, above all others, must be driven into the heart of the race—branded upon its mind. The account in Genesis was for moral and religious purposes. To serve these purposes in the best possible way, it was necessary that the account should be but an outline."

Numerous attempts have been made to show

that the account in Genesis is in fundamental harmony with the geological record by interpreting the word "day" as meaning an indefinitely long period of time. Such attempts are foredoomed to failure, in the opinion of the writer, because

1. The word for "day" (*yôm* in the Hebrew), is used in the Hebrew way for a period of twenty-four hours, as seen in the expression, "the evening and the morning were the first day," etc. It is a well-known fact that the Hebrews counted the day as beginning at sunset and continuing until the succeeding sunset. To obviate this difficulty, some have attempted to interpret the "evening" as referring to the "chaos" and "morning" as the "order" which emerged from it! However, the same word for day (*yôm*) is used in Genesis ii:2 and 3 where reference is made to the setting aside of the seventh day as a holy day because on that day the Lord rested from all His labors. Is it not likely that the force of the Sabbath-day injunction would be more impressive if *yôm* were taken in a literal sense, than if in the first six cases it was used to signify an indefinite, but very long period of time? Is it not clear that the author had his eye upon the *religious* significance of his narrative and not upon its *scientific* interpretation? Does it not appear to be more sensible, and to do less violence to the sense of the text to consider that the author of Genesis had no thought of giving a lesson in science?

2. The attempt to correlate the "days" of Genesis with the "periods" of geological time cannot

succeed. In the first place, the Biblical account limits the creation to *six* days. It is not possible to limit the geological periods to six, unless by combining some equally as distinct from each other as from those not included in such a "day." In the second place, the order of the appearance of plants and animals, not to speak of the sun and moon, cannot, by any process of combination or elimination, be made to accord with the geological record. For example, it is positively established that many different groups of animals, if indeed not all the "branches," had appeared before the "seed-bearing" plants; birds and whales, according to Genesis i: 21 were formed on the fifth day, while the reptiles were not produced until the sixth, whereas it is absolutely demonstrated by geology that the reptiles were in existence and flourished greatly before the birds appeared and both came in long before man, whom Moses states was formed on the same sixth day, though apparently at a later hour than reptiles.

It seems to the present author, that no violence is done to our religious feelings if, accepting the facts of geology, we still assert that the author of Genesis really intended to say what a literal interpretation of the text naturally leads one to think. The whole question is one of the "scriptural" rather than the "legalistic" method of interpretation, as Kershner uses those terms. We must look behind the words used to determine the "spirit" of the message. When that is done it becomes at once a clear and luminous message. The author of

Genesis has simply used a familiar law of pedagogy, that a thought to be impressed upon the mind of the learner must be couched in familiar terms; in language suited to his understanding. Such an interpretation does not in any way convict Moses of ignorance nor deceit. The account is not *untrue*. It is simply adapted to the understanding of the kindergarten class instead of university seniors.

The same method of interpretation avoids the difficulty inherent in the inconsistencies so obvious upon a comparison of the second account of creation in the second chapter of Genesis with that in the first. The author was intent upon deepening and indelibly fixing the idea of the One true God in the minds of the Hebrew people. He was dressing his real message in other words. He was intent also upon emphasizing the goodness of God to man in providing him with the fruits of the soil and the dominion over the lower animals. The account of Eve's creation teaches the essential unity of man and woman; the idea that she was bone of his bone and flesh of his flesh was a strong incentive to conjugal peace and happiness. It emphasizes God's plan for the establishment of the home, and no race perhaps has exemplified this more consistently than have the Hebrews.

The third chapter of Genesis teaches man's responsibility to his Maker and the nature of sin, *i.e.*, rebellion against His law and the consequences of disobedience. It also plainly teaches the lesson that innocence and virtue are not the same. Man could not become truly virtuous until he had the power of choice between good and evil. It is the choice of evil which causes man's fall; it is when man knowingly rejects the good and does the wrong, that he sins. Under the imagery so delightful to the oriental mind, this lesson is forcefully taught. This chapter is no more to be regarded as a dry philosophical discourse, than the first is to be considered a treatise on science. The Hebrew of that time could not have understood, nor likely would have accepted, the conclusions of a piece of abstract philosophical reasoning, but he could understand and did accept, at least in principle, the same conclusions when brought to him so concretely as in the account of the serpent in the Garden of Eden. It was a stroke of genius, if one will not acknowledge it as a divine inspiration from God, this thing of appealing to the *heart* of the unlearned Hebrew people, through a medium which they loved. The Semitic mind revelled in imagery; it mulled over and over, and gradually assimilated the underlying lessons which Moses intended it should.

Does this make out Moses a liar? Far from it; his technique was most artistic and refined. A bald statement of his theology would not have appealed to his hearers. He adapted his language to their habit of mind and to their understanding. With this interpretation, Genesis becomes at once one of the world's greatest wonders. No product of the human mind has ever surpassed it and none outside of the Bible has equalled it as a revelation of God's goodness and power. Is not this evidence of its divine inspiration? What more could be said?

Does the doctrine of evolution destroy the Book of Genesis? Has it not rather led to a fuller and deeper realization of the truly wonderful nature of the Book? Is not one's faith the deeper and do not the same fundamental truths remain and have a meaning for us today, though we no longer think as did our forefathers in the childhood days of the race? We need only to translate them into terms suited to our own age and degree of development. "When I was a child, I spake as a child, I understood as a child, I thought as a child," but now that I have become a man, let me put off, if needs be, the swaddling clothes of my childish fancies, and think as a man should think, clearly and deeply.

From this point of view, how many of the difficulties in the way of faith on the part of many sincere souls disappear! What has become of the supposed conflict between science and religion? Does it not becomes clear, in the words of J. Arthur Thomson, that:

"Science and Religion are incommensurables, and there is no true antithesis between them—they belong to different universes of discourse. Science is descriptive and offers no ultimate explanation; Religion is transcendental and interpretative, implying a realization of a higher order of things than those of sense-experience. . . . The so-called "conflict between science and religion" depends in part on a clashing of particular expressions of religious belief with facts of science, or on a clashing of particular supposedly scientific philosophies with religious feeling, or on attempts to combine in one statement scientific and religious formulations. . . . But the bulk of the conflict is due to a misunderstanding, to a false antithesis between incommensurables. While Science can give no direct support to religious convictions, because its province lies within the range of sense-perceptions, it establishes conclusions which religion may utilize, just as philosophy utilizes them, and transfigure, just as poetry transfigures them."

CHAPTER XIII

EVOLUTION AND CHRISTIANITY

IN a paper recently read before a "Congress" of one of the larger and more influential religious bodies in the United States, the following statements occur:
"It should be noted that one may be a theistic evolutionist and not be a Christian. It is anomalous to speak of Christian evolution. Evolution can never be made to harmonize with Christ. His early life began and ended in a miracle. The theistic evolutionist who is a Christian is compelled to minimize the importance of the miracles, to make light of their evidential value, and oftentimes deny them altogether, which is practically a denial of Christ himself." (W. N. Briney, "Evolution in Schools and Colleges," published in *The Christian Standard,* Cincinnati, Ohio, December 17, 1921.)

William Jennings Bryan not long ago delivered an address in which he said' "Now, I believe that everything that attacks belief in God is an enemy to the church, and because the church is a factor in civilization, is an enemy to civilization; and I want just for the moment here to lay before you one matter that has been on my heart. And that is the effect of the doctrine that has respectable authority behind it that is shaking the faith of the boys and girls in the Bible. And that is the doctrine that man, instead of being created by the Almighty, with a purpose and according to a plan, is nothing but a development from the lower animals. There are many who believe that that doctrine must be accepted. The fact that you can find no authority for it in the Bible ought to be sufficient to make a Christian hesitate before he accepts it. Take the word of God from the first verse of Genesis to the last of Revelation; there is not a sentence or a syllable that can be invoked to support the idea that man has in him the blood of the brute."

The question confronting us is this: Is the theory of evolution anti-Christian? Mr. Briney and Mr. Bryan, in company with many others, say that it is. Do the facts in the case bear out their contention?

One of the favorite devices of those who contend that "evolution is anti-Christian" is to cite examples of those who support an anti-Christian position by reliance on the atheistic philosophy which they supposedly draw from their belief in the doctrine of evolution. We have already shown that philosophically the materialistic position will not stand the test of careful scrutiny. Furthermore, materialistic philosophy is not only anti-Christian, it is anti-religious. The believer in the Koran or in Buddhism would call these same persons anti-Mahommedan, or anti-Buddhist. Atheism is due to a state of mind, which has always had a sporadic existence everywhere. The *genus* ex-

EVOLUTION AND CHRISTIANITY

isted long before the discovery of organic evolution; the *species* may have changed, but that is all! It is clearly not proper therefore to lay the blame for their atheism upon the doctrine of evolution. Once let the church perceive evolution as God's plan of creation and accept and teach it as such, and then it will be found that the atheists will have shifted the grounds for their unbelief to some other proposition. That atheistic materialists have used the doctrine of evolution in propagating their theory, it is not our purpose to deny. But Voltaire, who did not have the advantage of the later discovery of evolution to rely upon, used the theory of gravitation to the same end. In fact he made it the basis of his "skepticism"; but now who hears any one arguing that the law of gravitation has destroyed his faith in the Christian religion? The fact that some atheists who are also evolutionists have been so vociferous in proclaiming their views has had its effect, no doubt, in producing the wide-spread notion that evolution is necessarily anti-Christian. It is time that the many scientists who are not materialists should make known their philosophy and religious faith; they have perhaps been blameworthy in keeping silent under great provocation; but the average scientist hates the appearance of controversy. He is inclined to "keep cool"; to weigh questions of fact with deliberation and calmness of judgment; he is not of the temperament which leads one to mix in affairs where prejudice and pride of opinion are rampant.

Evolution and Christian Faith

The thoughtful evolutionist realizes fully that the Christian religion has a scientific basis in man's ethical nature. Its results have been subjected to centuries of living experiment and have stood the test as clearly and as fully as any other scientific fact. If for no other reason, a scientist, who really gives the matter the proper consideration, must conclude that the essentials of Christianity are true, for the very same reason that he accepts a theory as true in his own particular field, for example, the theory of evolution, namely, because "it works," that is, under specified conditions it brings about the specified results, or if it fails to do so in any particular case (experiment) it is because of a difference in the circumstances or factors involved. Accepting then the conclusion, as we feel we must, that the Christian religion is true and that evolution is an established fact, the two cannot be incompatible; evolution cannot be anti-Christian.

A thorough-going evolutionist, and at the same time, a devout and active Christian is the well-known dean of American botanists, Dr. John M. Coulter. In discussing this very point he says:

"The fact is that these two great fields (evolution and Christianity), so far from being contradictory, are mutually helpful. In this way the revelation of God in nature has supplemented His revelation through Christ. I find nothing more helpful to the student and leader of men than a clear appreciation of the working of evolution as exemplified in plants and animals. Evolution teaches that progress is gradual; that a better is progress toward the best; that sudden radical changes are not to be expected; that the future has its roots in the present. It teaches that revolutions are not the ordinary way of working, and that reformation may be very slow. It forbids unreasonable demands upon the individual or upon society, and discountenances the usual type of reformer. It shows that there have been no universal catastrophes and new creations, but that the present has gradually evolved from the past, and that the future will appear in the same gradual way. Furthermore, it shows that advance in a certain direction may not be uniform, for there are periods of apparent recession, as well as those of more rapid advance. The results are only apparent in the long view over long periods of time, when the tossing back and forth of surface waves disappears, and the steady advance of the slow-moving current becomes apparent.

"Perhaps most important of all, it teaches that man is a poor interpreter of individual events, and has no means of deciding whether they contribute to advance or not. Hence it must lead to cautious and charitable judgments; but at the same time it supplies a strong ground of confidence that there must be eventual progress. Some of the minor details of evolution may be useful to the pessimist, but its whole sweep justifies broad optimism. It is certainly true that the message of Christianity must not be imperilled by an ignorant contradiction of demonstrated facts. It is the Christian

EVOLUTION AND CHRISTIAN FAITH

claim that God has revealed Himself to man not merely in the words of Scripture, but also in the works of nature. It would seem likely, therefore, that the revelation of Scripture is supplementary to that of nature, containing further but not contradictory revelation. It would seem more logical, therefore, to read our knowledge of nature into our interpretation of Scripture, than to interpret nature by our conceptions of Scripture. The frequent attempts to interpret natural phenomena by conceptions derived from Scripture have so often ended disastrously that a reversal of the process might be suggested. That these disasters do not involve the Scriptures simply demonstrates that the conclusions were unessential."[1]

One other paragraph from Coulter is apropos to the character of the arguments set forth in the addresses of Mr. Briney and Mr. Bryan already referred to, and for that reason indulgence is craved for its quotation:

"The thoughtful Christian certainly appreciates the fact that the presentation of his religion must be adjusted to the increasing body of scientific truth. To hazard religion upon the issue involved in denying matters of definite experience is not to be thought of. In a scientific age the result would be to alienate the increasing thousands who have breathed the atmosphere of the modern laboratory, and to convert a powerful and helpful

[1] John M. Coulter, "Is Evolution Anti-Christian?", in *The Christian Century*, Chicago, Dec. 8, 1921, p. 12.

influence into a serious obstruction. One of the fundamental blunders of the old theological *régime* was its assumption of authority in connection with details of scientific thought. Grievous injury to the cause of Christianity has been done by *ex cathedra* statements in reference to the methods and doctrines of science by those who are not qualified to speak upon such subjects. For one to pass upon matters that belong to specialists in another field of investigation is to imperil his real message. . . . Any opinion based upon ignorance is essentially prejudiced and worthless, and must react unfavorably upon the cause it is claimed to represent. As Christians we must recognize in scientific investigation a very special field of work, whose announced results are to be received with respect and caution, and concerning the truth of which only scientific investigation is competent to decide."

The mistake made by practically all opponents of the doctrine of evolution is that of confusing the Darwinian theory of natural selection, or the survival of the fittest, with evolution itself. Moreover, recognition is given to only *one* of Darwin's factors, namely, to what may be called the *lethal* (death) factor. Huxley's pessimistic view of nature as a "gladiator's show," with every organism red in tooth and claw, ravenous and destructive as a wolf, seems to complete their conception of "evolution." "The cruel law under which the strong kill off the weak," "the law of hate" (Bryan), such are the expressions used. They overlook even in the Darwinian theory itself the fact that the survival of the fit does not mean necessarily the destruction of the individual, but rather want of success in the production of offspring. The opponents of "evolution" overlook entirely the factors of parental love and care, of sociality and cooperation among fellows of the same species; mutual aid has been at least as great a factor as strength and courage. In the words of J. Arthur Thomson ("Evolution," p. 248): "The ideal of evolution is thus no gladiator's show, but an Eden; and though competition can never be wholly eliminated—the line of progress is thus no straight line but at most an asymptote—it is much for our pure natural history to see no longer struggle, but love as 'creation's final law.'"

But if the Christianity of the New Testament is good and true, as we believe it is, the discoveries of science should not contradict it but complete its verification. "As a matter of fact they have been verifying it. The generalizations of physics and biology have verified the factor of truth in the doctrine of foreordination. The generalizations of biology and psychology have verified the factor of truth in the doctrine of inherited sin. And now, our latest psychology verifies the doctrine of regeneration. Experimentally it demonstrates that the Old Adam of inherited instinct (or original nature) can be dissociated from the stimuli that it has heretofore reacted to and associated with stimuli to which it will thenceforth react "in newness of life." Instincts, habits, imagination, intellectual reflection and purpose all can be "reconditioned," thereby renewing "the whole man." The renewing does not reach or affect the germplasm, it cannot be biologically transmitted to subsequent generations; to this extent the Old Adam survives, but each generation, after it is born, can be morally regenerated, in some degree." (F. H. Giddings, in an article in *The Independent*, August 20, 1921.)

Evolution is consistent with the doctrine that Christian character is a gradual growth and development. It teaches that strait and narrow is the way of salvation. It shows that those who sin against the Creator's laws must pay the penalty. Time and again have species no less than individuals sought the easy downward way that leads to extinction. Time and again has it been shown that only in the struggle against odds, in the choice of the path that tells for the good of the race rather than the immediate satisfaction of the individual desires, true progress and ultimate salvation lie. On all sides nature offers a choice between good and evil, and the reward or punishment is sure. This surely is the doctrine of New Testament Christianity.

The opponents of the doctrine of evolution sometimes assert the divinity and miraculous origin of Christ and in the same breath demand that evolution "account for Him." Now, but a moment's reflection is needed to see that the demand is preposterous. If the divinity of Christ be admitted, both He and His origin are at once removed entirely from the field of operation for evolution. Evolution is a law of nature; on the hypothesis of His relationship to the Godhead as set forth in the New Testament Scriptures, the Christ could not, in the usual sense of the term, be a part of nature. The Creator must have existed before the thing created, and in the Gospel according to John we are expressly told: "All things were made by Him; and without Him was not anything made that was made." Evolution therefore could have had no part in the production of a divine Christ. There is no precedent in nature, so far as we know, for the incarnation; it can only be accepted by the believer as a unique event; it is not to the discredit of the doctrine of evolution that it cannot account for Him.

Evolution is also asked to account for the miracles of Christ. The reply to this demand is implied in what has just been said. Here again the demand is for something which does not fall within the realm of evolution. Evolution does not limit the power of the Omnipotent One; it only expresses the method by which the Creator chose to work out the *creation of nature* in so far as it is manifest to finite minds. Who can say what other "laws" of God there may be, which are not operative in the field that is usually comprehended in the term "nature," and are therefore beyond the apprehension of the human mind? In fact, can human intellect actually apprehend the operation of any so-called "natural law?" Is it to be supposed, however, that the God of law and order, which all

EVOLUTION AND CHRISTIANITY

nature proclaims Him to be, would ever work in a "lawless" manner? Such an idea is repugnant to all revelations of the Divine Nature, which we possess.

Every observation and experience of man confirms him in the belief that God works only in accord with His own self-established laws. Is it probable, therefore, that in the recorded miracles of Christ, we may find infractions of God's laws? To ask the question is to answer it. Clearly, they could not have been infractions of the Divine laws. If the Spirit of God was incarnate in the Christ, then it was impossible for God to act contrary to His own rules of conduct, in connection with His wonderful works. But the Infinite comprehends not only those things known and understood by the finite, but also those beyond the comprehension of the human mind; otherwise there could be no Infinity. In this Infinite comprehension there is room for laws of which the mind of man has no inkling; they belong to the realm of the super-human, *i.e.*, to the realm beyond the power of man to control or understand. Any miracle of the divine Son of God, while it may seem to contravene the known laws of nature, must be therefore in accord with some higher law of which the human mind can at present, at least, form no conception.

The law of gravitation holds universally in nature; nothing has ever been known to "break" it. Yet it is possible to supersede the law of gravitation by other laws, the laws of aeronautics for example, and man flies in his heavier-than-air machines. A century ago the flight of a man, such a common sight today, would have been considered a "miracle"—a wonderful thing, in the literal significance of the term. But today, because we in a measure understand how it is done, it is not miraculous to us. The record of Christ's miracles is one of what are still and probably always will remain "wonderful" works to us, because they could only have been the result of knowledge which infinitely transcends our human powers; a knowledge which can employ forces by which the ordinary laws of nature may be put in abeyance, not broken. With the miracles, therefore, evolution has nothing to do.

The point is that evolution is confined to the mechanism of nature, and is but the tool of the Omnipotent One, the Spirit that operates in nature. It is His wheel, so to speak, on which He molds the plastic clay of the organisms into those forms He desires. The Christian Religion is concerned not with the mechanism of nature, but with our relation to the Spirit of God. Its plane of operation is a higher and totally distinct one. Evolution and Christianity therefore meet only in the operation of the Divine Will in man. *Evolution is God's method of operation in the realm of nature; Christianity is God's plan of operation in the spiritual world. The natural man, the product of the law of evolution, becomes transformed through the Gospel of Christ into spiritual accord with the Father, becomes the spiritual child of God by adoption, and thus attains the hope of personal immortality.*

The very least that could be said of the relation of evolution to Christianity would be that they are incommensurables, and as such evolution leaves the Christian Religion exactly where it has always been, *free to stand or fall upon the evidence for its divine origin.* The doctrine of evolution presents no difficulties too great to be harmonized with the gospel of Christ. It has no quarrel with His birth, life, death or resurrection. The theistic evolutionist is not "compelled to minimize the importance of the miracles, to make light of their evidential value or to deny them altogether." Theistic evolution does not attack a belief in God, but affords the strongest possible evidence of His existence. As the most potent evidence of a man is that of his works, so evolution, the method of God's work in nature, is potent evidence of the existence and power and wisdom of God. The doctrine of evolution cannot be an enemy of the church, if fairly received by those in ecclesiastical authority, for it aids and strengthens Christian faith and character. The doctrine of evolution teaches more than anything else that man is the culminating achievement in God's plan of creation; that it was by no mere chance that he arrived when and where he did, but that he had been foreseen and foreordained from the foundation of the world. The fact that the Bible does not distinctly teach the doctrine is not one to be counted against it, for there are many different doctrines which no one doubts to be true, which are not taught in the Bible, *because they, as well as evolution, are not germane to the purpose for which the Bible was written.*

The greatest error of theology has usually been a belated alliance with outgrown scientific theory. The theologian often lacks the training necessary to enable him to discern the current trend in scientific thought. This is exemplified clearly in his "discovery" of the weaknesses inherent in Darwinism—a condition of things known so long ago to biologists that they had passed on to the consideration of other more important matters. Unaware apparently of the true relation of Darwinism to the doctrine of evolution as it is understood by scientists today, the theologians, in some cases at least, seem unable to apprehend that science is a living, growing organism, and so they have dropped back to champion a dead and badly decayed scientific theory—that of special creation. Unless theology remains plastic enough to adapt itself to new knowledge, it fossilizes and loses its hold upon its day. This is the condition in which friends of religion find much of the current theology.

CHAPTER XIV

THE SWING OF THE PENDULUM

WHEN only a few years ago, in his thoughtful little volume, "A Critique of the Theory of Evolution" (p. 38), Professor Morgan wrote that the conflict between science and theology over the question of special creation *vs.* evolution had ended, and that it was unlikely that it would ever again be revived, he spoke neither as a prophet nor the son of a prophet! The year 1921 witnessed the unexpected revival of the old conflict in virulent form; nay, more, the calendar was turned back three centuries and even the old dispute over the form of the earth arose from the grave! In the city of Zion (Illinois) the school children are compelled by theological authority expressed through the civil government to learn that the earth is flat "like a pie, surrounded by a circle of water, inclosed by an outer circle of impenetrable ice!" In Kentucky, a board of education is reported to have dismissed a teacher from a position in the public schools because she taught that *the earth is round*; and this dismissal is said to have been supported by a decision of a court of law, to the effect that this teaching is contrary to the plain statement of the Bible, and therefore contrary to fact, and justifies the action of the school board! Furthermore, a "congress" composed of about seven hundred delegates from twenty-six states, representing one of the religious bodies among the more important in the United States on account of its numerical strength, devoted practically its whole time to a discussion of the prevalence of the teaching of evolution in its schools and colleges, and appointed a committee to investigate the situation with a view to the withholding of all financial support from such as might be found guilty of this "heresy." At least two state conventions of another religious body, even greater in number of communicants than that just referred to, took similar action, while the state of Kentucky came near enacting a law forbidding the teaching of this scientific doctrine in any school supported by public funds. The situation provokes one to wonder whether by some magic process the scroll of time may not have been turned back three centuries to the days of Copernicus and Galileo.

Those who have the deepest regard for the future welfare of the Christian religion cannot but hold grave fears for the outcome of this peculiar revival of the old, antiquated ideals and methods of the dark ages. History apparently has taught no lessons to those responsible for the present situation. At the very time when the church thinks she has discovered a wide-spread indifference to, if not dislike for, religion and the church, she attempts to make use of the very force which perhaps more than anything else has brought about the condition which so alarms her. As Paulsen ("An Introduction to Philosophy," page 335) has well said: "*Faith is by nature the tenderest, freest, and innermost function of life. It perishes as soon as constraint, the fear of man and politics come into play. That is the most evident of all the truths which the history of Western nations teaches.*" And yet it is a truth which, despite over three hundred years of American history, many of us have not learned. Our forefathers built our nation upon the foundation of religious liberty, of the separation between church and state; our generation is rushing pell-mell into the old condition of *a church-controlled state;* into the mediæval doctrine that all men must be forced by law to an outward conformity to an established form of religious dogma. Were the various denominations all harmoniously united, this might not be *practically* so serious a matter; there might be such unanimity of opinion as to secure the assent of the great majority to any such an enactment as that proposed in Kentucky. But with conditions what they are, such unanimity is impossible; the attempt to put such a principle into practice cannot but bring about strife and contentions; bitterness of feeling and possibly disturbance of the civil peace are not remote possibilities. *The principle is wrong.* Apparently one sect has almost sufficient political power in Kentucky today to write its own peculiar views into law. What is to hinder this same sect tomorrow, provided only it has a working majority in the state government, from passing a law compelling every man, woman, and child to do without the services of a regular physician in the treatment of bodily ailments, and to submit themselves only to some form of so-called "divine healing"? Did they but realize it, the fundamental sciences upon which the practice of medicine is based are themselves grounded upon the doctrine of evolution! Is it too much to expect that in the near future, therefore, Kentucky will forbid the practice of medicine?

A true religion, or rather, a true view of religion will "not demand that we think what cannot be thought, but that we believe what satisfies the heart and the will, and does not contradict reason" (Paulsen, p. 334). The estrangement between many minds, trained in science, and the church "is evidently due to the fact that religion has been converted into a pseudo-scientific system for whose formulæ an unqualified recognition is demanded. The spirit of freedom and the more sensitive theoretical conscience of modern times rebels against the attempt to subject it to such dogmas constructed by human hands. It has been customary to lay infidelity on the wickedness of the will which refuses to be subjected to a wholesome discipline. Perhaps there is some truth in the saying. But it would be wilful self-delusion to attribute all estrangement from the church and all opposition to faith to this cause" (Paulsen, p. 334).

The attempt to forbid any certain doctrine by civil law is unfortunate not only because of the union of church dogma with state enactment, but also because it will alienate many of the sincerest believers in Christianity who are convinced of the truth of both that religion and the scientific doctrine of evolution. Most of these are persons of keen minds, deep thought, and earnestness of purpose; they are just the type of individual whom the church can least afford to lose. Were it a matter vital to Christianity, it might be comprehensible that the church would take just the stand that some of her misguided adherents are taking; but such is not the case. Religion in general, and Christianity in particular, "does not rest upon a hypothesis concerning the origin of living beings, any more than it rests upon a definite idea of the astronomical form of the world. Its concern with such matters, if it has any at all, is only with the objective truth and subjective truthfulness of our knowledge. What is dangerous to it as well as to all things human is the alliance with error and falsehood. The church ought to have learned so much at least from her unfortunate conflict with modern cosmology in the seventeenth century, that *it is under no circumstances advisable for her to affiliate with any scientific system.* When the church made the Aristotelian-Ptolemaic cosmology an article of faith, she applied the axe to the roots of her faith. *Every blow that struck the false theory also struck the church. The same effect is bound to ensue if the church declares a certain biological view as part of her doctrine.* The persons who see in Darwinism the final destruction of religion well illustrate this fact. By removing the Mosaic account of creation, and Adam and Eve, they say, Darwin has, at the same time, made superfluous for biology, "the hypothesis of a God." . . . From youth many have been taught to regard the existence of God as proved and assured by the teleological argument; now they no longer have confidence in the old proof and consequently reject the thing itself. Nothing is more dangerous to a good cause than false arguments" (Paulsen, p. 158). These words are peculiarly apropos today in this country, though written in a foreign land over a quarter of a century ago.

The state of mind of one who has lost his religious faith because of some scientific doctrine is "evidently preconditioned by the original intellectualistic bent of his religious convictions, formed by his early instruction. He has a feeling of having been cheated by false theories and proofs, and therefore looks with distrust upon the entire church. This is an everyday occurrence. The mutual distrust existing between science and the church is fatal to her. *The proper attitude for her, however, does not consist in always accepting the latest theories, but in making herself altogether independent of scientific and philosophical theories. What I offer, she must say, is valid, whether Copernicus or Ptolemy, Darwin or Agassiz, is right. The gospel is and has no system of cosmology and biology; it preaches the kingdom of God which is to be realized in the heart of man.*" (Paulsen, p. 160). Thus speaks one of the greatest thinkers among the devout philosophers of our time.

The question arises from a contemplation of the current situation whether those, who think themselves doing God's service in thus striving by legal enactment to preserve their own peculiar views, may not be putting themselves in the position of Saul of Tarsus before his conversion on the way to Damascus. In his persecution of the early church Saul sincerely believed that he had the complete and hearty approval of the God whom he worshipped with all the strength of his soul. Yet when the scales had fallen from his eyes, he was convinced of his mistaken point of view and no one more consistently strove to advance the kingdom against which he had formerly been in opposition. His persecution of the Christians in his earlier manhood was due to his false conception of Christianity and his mistaken theology. May not some of our modern theologians find themselves unwittingly standing in Paul's old shoes? All that Christian theology needs is the affirmation of the origin of mankind in God, irrespective of the process by which he was produced. Enlightened theologians, such as Dr. William Newton Clarke (see his "Outline of Christian Theology," p. 224) admit this. But apparently the church as a whole has not outgrown the old custom of offering "definite statements concerning the time and manner of origin of the human race, and to consider such statements indispensable to its positions concerning religion. With the same view of its duty it has also been accustomed to offer definite statements concerning the time and manner of the origin of the earth, and to regard its own independent view of the creation of the world as indispensable to its religious teaching" (*loc. cit.*). Perhaps it is safe to say that a majority of the Bible students today have readjusted their thinking to accord with the discoveries of astronomy and geology, and are convinced that theology can safely leave this problem to these sciences, since, no matter what the process may have been, it must have been God's method. "Accordingly, Christian theology no longer maintains," says Clarke, "that the earth was created in six days, or at the date to which the genealogies in Genesis lead back, but gives its assent to the antiquity of the planet and the method by which worlds generally have been formed." He maintains the view that Christian theology, far from suffering any loss, is actually the gainer by the change in view, since it "relieves theology of the consideration of a question that is not essential to its own sole work."

Pursuing the matter further, Dr. Clarke finds also that "what is true of the earth is true of the human race. . . . The time has come when theology should remand the investigation of the time and manner of the origin of man to the science of anthropology with its kindred sciences, just as now it remands the time and manner of origin of the earth to astronomy and geology, and should accept and use their discoveries on the subject, content with knowing that the origin of mankind, as of all else, is in God." This attitude is in perfect harmony with the principles of theology, since it proclaims the *unity* of God. "If God is one, what He has taught in one place is to be received as loyally as what He has taught in another. The history of man, like the history of other denizens of the earth, is to be learned through investigations of all ascertainable facts; and it is impossible that God should have intended ever to contradict the testimony of facts by any utterance in words." Hence, Dr. Clarke reaches a conclusion that apparently cannot be avoided, namely, that this is a scientific or historical question which is to be investigated freely by the scientifico-historical method, and the truth discovered in this way "must be accepted and admitted to influence when it has been ascertained." He willingly and freely admits, what seems so clear to one who examines the evidence without prejudice or bias, that "there is a testimony from the sciences that investigate the origin of mankind, so definite and well-established as to demand recognition in the field of theology, as well as in the intelligent world at large."

Moreover, this situation gives reason on the part of theology for self-congratulation, since she may now lay aside an inquiry no longer found to be essential for her purposes. Religion cannot be made to depend upon any method of origin of man more than upon that of the world. Man has "his position and standing among living things, and no theory of the manner of his origin can make him other than he is. He will always be a dependent being, in whose life religion is a normal and necessary element." He "is a part of the one great system in which the eternal creative power and purpose have been progressively manifested. Man is the crown of the system, . . . a spirit capable of communing with his holy and gracious Creator. In the entire process the crowning conception, *man,* has been always in view, and toward him the great movement has steadily advanced. . . . Man is not lowered to an inferior level occupied by nature, but nature is raised to a higher grade by having man for its supreme outcome. Man, the crown of the process, is no mere animal, but a spiritual being of vast powers, high destinies and incomparable needs, whose life in God is religion."

Dr. Clarke apparently supports the view set forth in a preceding chapter of this book (see *The Embryology of the Mind*) that there is no more reason for postulating a special creation of the soul of man than of his body—*"not because there is no need of God for the producing of the human soul, but because there is so much of God in the perpetual travail of creation that even this marvellous addition to existence is sufficiently accounted for already by His presence in the process.* Christianity can accept and employ this solution of the question of origins as well as the one that was formerly received. Theology will be altered in some respects by such a change, but not destroyed nor even revolutionized. . . . *There is no ground for foes to hope or friends to fear that*

THE SWING OF THE PENDULUM

Christianity must retire if the evolutionary idea gains entrance. God is still the Creator and Lord, man is bound to Him in obligation, sin is in the human race, and the divine grace in Christ is still the hope of the world" (p. 226).

SUGGESTED READINGS

THE following list of books is by no means exhaustive but is rather a suggestion for a course of reading for those who desire to pursue the subject farther than could be done in the present volume. The arrangement is that which will probably be found most logical, beginning with those of a general introductory nature and gradually progressing to those more extensive or more technical in nature. Many of these works contain bibliographies which will lead the reader farther and farther into this field.

1. *Introduction to Science,*
    J. ARTHR THOMSON.
    Henry Holt and Co.

2. *The Theory of Evolution,*
    W. B. SCOTT.
    The Macmillan Co.

3. *Evolution,*
    GEDDES AND THOMSON.
    Henry Holt and Co.

4. *Readings in Evolution, Genetics and Eugenics,*
    H. H. NEWMAN.
    The University of Chicago Press.

5. *The Doctrine of Evolution,*
    H. E. CRAMPTON.
    Columbia University Press.

6. *Darwin and After Darwin,*
    G. J. ROMANES.
    The Open Court Publishing Co.

7. *Organic Evolution,*
    R. S. LULL.
    The Macmillan Co.

8. *Darwinism To-Day,*
    V. L. KELLOGG.
    Henry Holt and Co.

Evolution and Christian Faith

9. *The Origin of Species,*
    Charles Darwin.
    D. Appleton and Co.

10. *The Descent of Man,*
    Charles Darwin.
    D. Appleton and Co.

11. *The Direction of Human Evolution,*
    E. G. Conklin.
    Charles Scribner's Sons.

12. *Men of the Old Stone Age,*
    H. F. Osborn.
    Charles Scribner's Sons.

13. *The Interpretation of Nature,*
    C. L. Morgan.
    The Macmillan Co.

14. *The Foundations of Zoology,*
    W. K. Brooks.
    The Macmillan Co.

15. *Why the Mind Has a Body,*
    C. A. Strong.
    The Macmillan Co.

16. *The Science of Human Behavior,*
    M. Parmalee.
    The Macmillan Co.

17. *Introduction to Philosophy,*
    Friedrich Paulsen; translated by Frank Thilly.
    Henry Holt and Co.

18. *An Outline of Christian Theology,*
    William Newton Clark.
    Charles Scribner's Sons.

www.ingramcontent.com/pod-product-compliance
Lightning Source LLC
Chambersburg PA
CBHW051910160426
43198CB00012B/1830